Touching God

Experiencing Metaphors for the Divine

Also by Ellyn Sanna
published by Paulist Press

Motherhood: A Spiritual Journey

Touching God

Experiencing Metaphors for the Divine

Ellyn Sanna

Paulist Press
New York/Mahwah, N.J.

Cover design by Cynthia Dunne
Interior artwork by Eileen Herb
Book design by Lynn Else

Library of Congress Cataloging-in-Publication Data

Sanna, Ellyn, 1958-
    Touching God : experiencing metaphors for the divine / by Ellyn Sanna.
        p. cm.
    Includes bibliographical references.
        ISBN 0-8091-4022-5
    1. God. 2. Metaphor—Religious aspects—Catholic Church. I. Title.
    BT103 .S26 2002
    231—dc21
                                                                    2002006700

Published by Paulist Press
997 Macarthur Boulevard
Mahwah, New Jersey 07430

www.paulistpress.com

Printed and bound in the
United States of America

Contents

Dedication

To Marietta
with gratitude
for all the ways you've helped me touch God's skin.

Introduction

You may not be able to define God in philosophical terms. Men through the ages have tried to talk about him. (Yes) Plato said that he was the Architectonic Good. Aristotle called him the Unmoved Mover. Hegel called him the Absolute Whole....We don't need to know all these high-sounding terms. (Yes) Maybe we ought to know him and discover him another way. (Oh yeah) One day you ought to rise up and say, "I know him because he's a lily of the valley." (Yes) He's a bright and morning star. (Yes) He's a rose of Sharon. He's a battle-ax in the time of Babylon. (Yes) And then somewhere you ought to just reach out and say, "He's my everything. He's my mother and my father. He's my sister and my brother. He's a friend of the friendless." This is the God of the universe.

—MARTIN LUTHER KING, JR.

The picture is a symbol: but it's truer than any philosophical theorem (or, perhaps, than any mystic's vision) that claims to go behind it.

—C. S. LEWIS

The story goes something like this:

A little girl couldn't sleep one night because the shadows in her bedroom looked long and dark. Frightened, she begged her parents to let her join them in their bed where she knew she would be safe. But her parents assured her she would be fine in her own room.

"After all," they said, "God is with you even when you are alone. Won't that help you not be afraid?"

The little girl shook her head. "Sometimes," she replied, "I need someone with skin on."

I can relate. Sometimes God seems too intangible, a brilliant and blurry concept I can't even wrap my intellect around, let alone clutch with my flesh-and-blood fingers. This God-concept is one I like to play with intellectually; the notion intrigues me, and theology fascinates me. But how does it change who I am as I move through the years firmly connected to a body? My life is full of tangible distractions: the noise of children's laughter, the telephone, and my own voice shouting in exasperation; the recurring patterns of hormones and meal times, paychecks and deadlines; the clutter of ambitions and unsorted mail, relationships and dirty laundry. Does God's abstract, incorporeal concept have any concrete effect amid all this? Is his influence real—or merely imaginary?

When I was a child, my world teemed with invisible friends, and God was as real as any of them. He ran at my side as I galloped on pretend horses across the endless, open prairie of my imagination. At some point, though, as I grew older, I began to doubt this loving God whom I touched only with the fingers of my imagination. Obviously, after all, make-believe isn't real.

Which left me with the other image of God I had lived with all my life, a narrow, tightfisted God whose favorite word was "No." Eventually, as an adolescent, I began to also believe in a God of mystery and light. I worshiped his hazy golden image for years, even while the negative tyrant-God kept his hard grip on my life.

My contradictory theology worked well enough until life got more complicated. Abstract notions, no matter how luminous and lovely, don't seem to help much when we face life's everyday sorrows and occasional emergencies, the traumas the passage of time brings to us all sooner or later. And a God who thinks we're bad offers an even more meager comfort.

In the end, I became disillusioned with both the abstract image of God and the disapproving one. Most of my life I had taken my faith for granted; now that I had lost it, I could think of nothing else. I wanted a God with definite outlines, a God to grab and touch—and I didn't believe he existed. I wanted a sign, some definite empirical proof that God was real, but I believed only psychotics thought they could truly see and hear God. Emotionally, I felt as though I were experiencing a hunger so real and painful that it consumed my life. And at the same time, intellectually, I had reached the conclusion that not only was there no food in sight, but food in fact was a delusion, a pretty fantasy with no basis in reality.

Lately, I've edged my way back to faith, grasping any handhold I can find to pull myself along. Some of these handholds are intellectual, some emotional, but one that seems to span the distance between my mind and heart is the language of poetry and literature. T. S. Eliot speaks of God in a pattern of metaphor and image that brings goose bumps to my skin; Annie Dillard strings together sentences describing nature's brutality and somehow ends up with a statement of faith; Madeleine L'Engle uses words to create a fantasy world my heart tells me has to be real. All this seems like proof of something, something amazing and reassuring that goes beyond rational argument and convinces the frightened child that huddles inside me.

When I was still deep in despair, a paragraph from C. S. Lewis's *Pilgrim's Regress* jumped out at me, where God speaks to the pilgrim of how the divine is revealed through both the senses and the imagination:

> It is but truth, not fact: not image, not the very real….this is the veil under which I have chosen to appear even from the first until now. For this end I made your senses and for this end your imagination, that you might see my face and live.

Truth does not equal fact; something imaginary may also be real. These concepts were like the first whiff of breakfast after a long, hungry night.

God, I realize now, is not the only one too slippery to grasp and hold. Actually, we can't grab hold of any concept unless we use analogies and symbols. "My love is like a red, red rose": This is a truth, a way to touch the unknowable reality of the person I love. And I would be foolish to be disillusioned with my love merely because I discovered he was neither red nor scented, that, in fact, in any literal sense, he was not particularly roselike at all. The line of poetry is not factual, not in the least. But in the world of the imagination, it is symbolically true.

Carl Jung said that a human being

> never perceives anything fully or comprehends anything completely. He can see, hear, touch, and taste; but how far he sees, how well he hears, what his touch tells him, and what he tastes depend upon the number and quality of his senses. These limit his perceptions....By using scientific instruments he can partly compensate for the deficiencies of his senses [but]...no matter what instruments he uses, at some point he reaches the edge of certainty beyond which conscious knowledge cannot pass.

So how can we peek out beyond certainty's edge? Jung concluded that we can only do it with symbols, with metaphors and images and fantasies. I had been desperately searching for a sign, something concrete and literal that would prove God's existence, but according to Jung, *symbols,* not signs, are what show us the unknowable. A sign can be literally translated into something comprehensible—like a company logo; like the Freudian interpretation of reality that equates keys and penises, mountains and breasts. But a symbol helps us grasp some truth that is humanly incomprehensible; it allows us to prove something that has no literal explanation.

A bolt of lightning from the sky; a bright-winged, white-robed angel bringing God's message; a talking donkey; or a burning bush: all these were biblical *signs* of God's presence. But in our world today I suspect the signs God gives us are few and far between.

Introduction

Symbols are a whole other story. Symbols are the stuff of which the sacraments are made, those tangible moments that celebrate an intangible mystery. Sacraments, my friend Sister Lois tells me, are outward signs of inner grace; but they are more than mere signs, for the external, empirical acts have been animated by something invisible and incomprehensible. They reach past the deficiencies of our senses.

I grew up in a religious tradition that looked at the sacraments as similes. A *simile,* we all remember from seventh-grade English, is a figure of speech that compares two very different things using the words *like* or *as.* And when the pastor handed out the tiny cubes of soft white bread, what he really meant to say was, "This is *like* the body of Jesus." He would never have said it actually *was* Jesus' body.

Since then I have been attracted to other faith traditions that see the sacraments as *metaphors*—a word that came from the Greek concept of transferring meaning from one thing to another. And so in the churches I tend to seek out now, what the priest is really saying is this: "This silvery white wafer that tastes like nothing at all *is* the body of Jesus."

I suspect, though, that either way, some mysterious intangible reality is carried from one thing to the other. As a child, I would have thought the concept of "eating Jesus" was a strange one—but I still understood that this small solemn meal meant something bigger, something more than just a bite of bread and a sip of grape juice. Somehow, the symbol is saturated with meaning.

And it is not only the seven officially recognized sacraments that work like this; all of life can be "sacramental." Here at last I find the answer to my question: The abstract, the incorporeal, does touch my everyday life in concrete ways. If my faith is rooted in my physical life, then it becomes as practical and serviceable as bread and light are— and my life, the whole mixed bag of beauty and frustration, joy and grief, becomes a concrete expression of something I will never see or hear or touch or smell.

Some days (many days, if I'm honest) this insight continues to elude me. Maybe my mind is too steeped in the paradigms of Western philosophy, believing only in what I can prove through the scientific method. Or maybe I'm simply too busy with the here and now to grasp the reality of something further and forever. But when my own faith falters once again, I'm comforted by the fact that centuries of poets and mystics have committed their hearts and intellects to this same insight with which I struggle.

Coleridge wrote that a symbol "partakes of the reality which it renders intelligible"—and thus God is transcendent in the "incidents and situations of common life." Gregory Palamas, a fourteenth-century theologian, said we can know God, because we apprehend "the transcendent reality figured forth symbolically." A sign, says Madeleine L'Engle, merely points the way, while a symbol (what she calls an "icon") contains something of the quality that it represents; it is "an open door to God." According to Thomas Aquinas, "Creatures can be called God's words." And Julian of Norwich wrote in her *Showings*, "The fullness of joy is to behold God in everything."

But it's hard to find God's face everywhere. Sometimes the symbol itself distracts us from any other reality that might whisper through it. Some metaphors don't speak to us at all. And when they speak most clearly, we wonder whether we're not simply hearing the voice of our own imagination, for most of us have learned that our imagination can be the source of delusion as well as revelation.

In the face of these dilemmas, we often end up confused and discouraged. We're like very young children, alone in a strange place, trying in vain to find some hint of our mother's presence.

But that's why a baby creates a security blanket for herself. Child psychologists call the blanket a "transitional object," something soft and warm that speaks to the child of the mother's gentleness and love. My three children each had some form of transitional object: a tattered quilt; a well-worn cloth doll; a small, sleep-stained pillow. They used these objects to bring themselves the same sense of comfort and security they drew from me; these inanimate things allowed my children to withstand being physically alone until they could internalize their own sense of safety and well-being.

Of course the quilt or doll or pillow only had meaning because my child gave it meaning; from a literal perspective, a piece of fabric is not much like a mother. And yet a security blanket is not a lie. The mother does exist, and she does love her child. The blanket simply allows the child to carry that love with her in a way she can touch and smell and feel. The blanket allows the baby to put skin on something that is intangible.

And now, as I look at my life, I see "transitional objects" everywhere I turn, ordinary things that speak to me of God's love. Nor are these symbols unique to my own vision; down through the centuries humans have seen God as a lover and a friend, a bird and a vine, a rock and living water.

Some mystics, however, point out that God cannot be contained by any of these symbols. These mystics' approach is called the *via negativa,* the way of emptiness and darkness that turns away from all metaphors for God and seeks to find him without words or images, without the distraction of anything tangible. The Old Testament authors also warned against confining God to a visual shape: "On the day when the Lord spoke to you out of the fire on Horeb," they reminded the Israelites, "you saw no figure of any kind" (Deut 4:15 NEB); Isaiah wrote that "those who make idols are less than nothing; all their cherished images profit nobody" (44:9). In other words, don't try to draw God's outline; don't limit him by turning him into something that can be seen and touched.

I am as guilty of this as anyone. Eternal, unconditional love is so incomprehensible that the concept fits awkwardly inside my brain; a finite God of my own creation, an idol, is much more convenient. Idols are more portable; I can tuck them neatly into whatever niche in my life is currently available. But an infinite Being tends to shatter all the cozy pigeonholes.

God is an iconoclast, constantly destroying our images of him. "If an icon becomes more important to us than what it reveals of God," Madeleine L'Engle writes, "then it becomes a golden calf." Golden calves are concrete and dependable, of course, knowable and controllable; but when we touch God's warm, living skin, those hard, cold images tend to topple. The process is seldom comfortable, but can you blame God? Something would be seriously wrong if a child preferred an inanimate blanket to a living relationship with an actual mother. Like any loving mother, God wants us near and healthy.

But most of us aren't ready to give up the blanket altogether. God is not limited to the boundaries of the physical world; yet his Spirit indwells creation, and we find him everywhere we turn. I suspect we all need some balance between the *via negativa* and its opposite, the *via positiva*.

From the very beginning, even the Bible's writers used metaphor after metaphor to bridge the gap between the invisible world and the ordinary visible one in which we live. God is a shield, they wrote (Gen 15:1), a rock (Deut 32:4), a king (Isa 52:7), a husband (Isa 53:5), a father (Isa 64:8), a mother (Isa 66:13), a shepherd (Ps 80:1). Jesus himself used all sorts of concrete symbols to help people grasp his reality; he called himself bread and light, a gate and a vine, a mother hen and a bridegroom.

Christ, after all, was the ultimate metaphor for God. He *was* God with skin on. But he told his disciples, "It is for your own good that I am going away. Unless I go away, the Counselor will not come to you....When the Counselor comes, whom I will send to you from the Father, the Spirit of truth who goes out from the Father, he will testify about me....[he] will teach you all things and will remind you of everything I have said to you" (John 16:7; 15:26; 14:26). The Spirit of Jesus is not confined to a single human body; he teaches us through all creation, including things as ordinary as food and water, housewives and farmers.

As for me, I find I catch a glimpse of his Spirit in my husband's arms and my friends' voices, in wind and earth, in plants and light. These metaphors have personal meaning within the intimate context of my current life, but that meaning depends on both my own past and on the traditions of generations. In all our lives, the particular and the universal weave together to give these symbols power.

Introduction

The material world shows us God—and the Spirit of truth breathes through creation, making the smallest seed significant. Like Moses, we cannot see God's face and live—but through a hundred daily metaphors we touch his skin.

> *To forbid the making of pictures about God would be to forbid thinking about God at all, for man is so made that he has no way to think except in pictures.*
>
> —DOROTHY SAYERS

> *Will you, God, really live with people on earth? Why, the heavens cannot contain you.*
>
> —1 KINGS 8:27–29

Metaphors from the Natural World

God, who made heaven and earth, the sea,
and everything in them...never left himself
without a witness. There were
always his reminders....

—ACTS 14:15, 17 NLT

1

Rock

On Christ the solid Rock I stand.
All other ground is sinking sand.

—EDWARD MOTE, 1797–1874

The foolish man built his house upon the sand
And the rains came a-tumbling down.
The rains came down and the floods came up,
And the house upon the sand fell flat!

The wise man built his house upon the rock
And the rains came a-tumbling down.
The rains came down and the floods came up,
And the house upon the rock stood firm!

—CHILDREN'S GOSPEL CHORUS

I grew up singing these songs in church and Sunday school. Hand motions went along with the gospel chorus; we children would mime we were hammering nails as we built our houses, and then we'd flutter our arms up and down for the falling rain and rising flood. We'd end with a clap when the foolish man's house fell flat. The wise man's verse, however, ended with our hands clasped tight together, demonstrating the solidness of the house on the rock.

As a child, I understood the song's symbolism: I knew that God was the Rock on which wise people built their lives. I suppose I assumed that building my house on God would mean "obeying the

Bible": in other words, "following all the rules." The image of a house falling flat was a frightening one, so of course I would rather have a house that stood firm—but nevertheless, the rock in my mind was a barren crest of stone. A house perched on such a rugged crag might be a bit precarious, I couldn't help but think; no matter how solid the rock, might not the house simply slip off those cold, sheer sides? And what would happen to me if I failed to keep all the rules? I had the reputation of being a "good girl"—but deep in my heart I hid the secret knowledge that I wasn't good at all. I broke the rules as much as anyone; I just didn't let anyone know I did. Would my life's little house slide off that stern solid rock and fall in a shattered pile?

The metaphor didn't quite work for me. A smaller stone might have shown my childish imagination the delight of divine permanence. I understood the wonder of pebbles that would not dissolve or break, and I was fascinated with the tiny unexpected treasures I found in my father's heap of gravel behind our house. I would have been surprised—and probably enchanted—if someone had suggested I was searching for God out in the gravel. With an image like that, I wouldn't have felt as though I were apt to fall off God's steep sides; instead, I might have realized I could keep him in my child's pocket and carry him with me. Even if I failed to follow all the rules, I could still clutch him tight between my fingers.

My seven-year-old daughter knows treasures lie hidden in the rocky creek bed near our house. Today, walking with her, at first my grown-up eyes saw only silt-colored rock; her sharp little fingers pointed out the delicate ridged prints of ancient shells, the glitter of mica flakes, the perfect angles of quartz crystals. She cried with delight as she spied each one, offered it to me for my inspection, then put it in her baseball cap. When the hat was full, she dropped down beside me, the stones in her lap, and contentedly examined each one again.

Later, my husband complained that odd bits of shale and flint have a tendency to find their way from her pockets to the corners of the bathroom, the kitchen counter, and the interior of the dryer. How can I say anything when beneath my own bed I keep two wooden cigar boxes, filled with favorite stones from my childhood? And by my computer are two pebbles from Lake Erie, gifts for my fifteenth birthday from my best friend. One is a jade-green stone the shape of a small pear, the other a smooth silver-gray, quartered by two pale rings. Through all my life's moves, from my parents' house to college dorms to apartments to the homes of my married life, I have kept these stones with me. Their hard shapes are reassuring and familiar between my fingers. In a world full of change, a world that seems frantically plastic and impermanent, these stones are tiny still points. Nothing endures but mutability, says the poet Shelley, but in the midst of the natural world's shifting cycles of loss and renewal, rock remains solid. It endures.

Last weekend I ran away from my responsibilities to a cemetery where the stones stood gray and quiet against the trees' vivid green. In a sheltered hollow I sat beside the graves of Gillie and Margaret MacFerson, born in the 1870s, died in the 1940s. "Beloved in life, cherished in death," reads Gillie's stone; "Safe in God's hands," affirms Margaret's.

The women are dead of course; their quick fingers, the tumble of words from their mouths, the flash of their eyes: All these the earth will never witness again. Only the blocks of granite endure. The Latin root of the word *endure* means both "hard" and "lasting," and things that are hard—like stone—tend to last longer than softer, more delicate things—like flesh and blood. And yet these gravestones affirm the truth: The names of Gillie and Margaret are still important; these women are real; they are loved.

For centuries, someone told me recently, Jews have left small stones for each prayer they offer at a person's grave. Gradually, the stones accumulate into rows and heaps, prayer and love made tangible and lasting. I like that. My memories and prayers are such fleeting things, so ephemeral that I wonder if they possess reality at all. I'd like to think I could use each thought to build something solid, something

5

permanent. That day in the cemetery, as I escaped my routine life, the MacFerson sisters' hard gravestones beneath my hands comforted me. Something in life is immutable.

The Old Testament authors drew the obvious connection: In our transient, mortal lives, Yahweh's consistent love is like a rock. In the Book of Second Samuel, when David is delivered from his enemies, he sings:

> The Lord is my rock, and my fortress, and my deliverer.
> The God of my rock; in him will I trust. (22:2)

And Psalm 62:5–6 says:

> He only is my rock and my salvation;…I shall not be moved. In God is…the rock of my strength.

Like stone, God offers stability, security, reliability.

But I can't escape the fact that this metaphor is not completely positive. Stone is unbending, unfeeling, infertile. Sitting on Gillie and Margaret MacFerson's graves, my abstract grief may be comforted by the solid touch of rock against my palm—but if Gillie and Margaret were people I had known and loved, cold stone would be a poor substitute for warm, yielding flesh. The hot, fragile color of blood and tissue makes life unbearably dear. Could I really love a God who was eternally the hard chilly gray of granite?

But the Old Testament story of Meribah tempers the rock metaphor with the strange, brilliant touch of paradox: At Meribah "the children of Israel strove with the Lord.…And Moses lifted up his hand, and with his rod he smote the rock twice; and the water came out abundantly, and the congregation drank, and their beasts also" (Num 20:13, 11). Stone is lifeless and unmoving; water is life-giving and flowing. Here these two opposites are joined together in a single metaphor.

The song of Moses in Deuteronomy 32 goes still further. Verse 4 says of Yahweh: "He is the Rock, his work is perfect; for all his ways are justice; a God of truth…." And then, with a startling twist of words, the author adds to this image of stern purity and unbending righteous masculinity another picture: "So the Lord…made him suck honey out of the rock, and oil out of the flinty rock" (vv. 12, 13). Not only does water flow from the divine Rock, but honey—nourishment and sweetness—and oil—a food, a fuel for lamps, a medicine for wounds, and a symbol of joy and honor. Like a woman giving birth, suddenly the Rock has burst open.

Apparently, God cannot be contained in a single, consistent symbol. When I think of him, I must mix my metaphors, I must allow for contradiction and paradox. Although he is enduring and eternal, "the same yesterday, today, and forever," yet over and over he leaps out at me in some new, vivid form, like treasure hidden in a heap of gravel.

When my oldest daughter was about a year old, I remember sitting at my in-laws' table offering her a peach. She sucked greedily at the soft flesh, juice dripping down her chin.

"Watch out for the stone." My father-in-law spoke English as his second language, and he meant the pit. "Don't let her choke on it," he cautioned.

My daughter clutched the "stone" in her sticky fist and refused to part with it. It came home with us and ended up in a basket with all the other odd bits of things I tend to collect.

And then, months later, on an impulse I poked the small hard lump into a flowerpot of soil. By this time, my father-in-law had died and was buried beneath his own gray piece of granite. But inside the pot, the peach pit sent out a tiny green shoot that poked up through the dirt. The stone had cracked open and sprouted life.

Rock of Ages, cleft for me,
Let me hide myself in Thee.

—AUGUSTUS MONTAGUE TOPLADY, 1776

Touching God

One day I saw with the eyes of my eternity
in bliss and without effort, a stone.
This stone was like a great mountain
and was assorted colors.

. . .

I asked the sweet stone: Who are you?
It replied: "I am Jesus."

—MECHTILD OF MAGDEBURG

2
Wind

When the day of Pentecost was fully come…there came a sound from heaven like a rushing mighty wind, and it filled all the house where they were sitting….And they were all filled with the Holy Spirit.

—ACTS 2:1–3 KJV

But because the Lord is Spirit, He blows where He wills.

—ORIGEN

When my children were young, I tried to pack my professional life and my mothering into the same geographical and temporal space. This meant that both my days and my home were crammed with a conflicting jumble of diapers and books, Play-Doh and file folders, crayons and computer discs. It meant that I was immersed in breast-feeding and make-believe at the same time I was establishing myself in my career. "How wonderful you have a job that allows you to stay home with your children," people said to me, their voices tinged with varying degrees of approval and envy. I would smile and nod: I loved my babies; I loved my work. I seldom expressed, even to myself, how brutal the demands of each were to the other.

How could I take time to listen to my children's voices when I had a deadline to meet? How could I find inspiration to create my professional work when I had spent my day cleaning up Cheerios and spilled juice, washing five loads of laundry, and reading Dr. Seuss so many times that my thoughts formed automatically into rhymes? I fiercely wanted to do well at both my roles, both professional and

9

maternal. And some days it worked: I somehow pulled together the two conflicting currents of my life and found joy in both. Other days I felt as though my life were a box so full of other people's demands there was no air left for me to breathe.

On one of those days, when I felt I might suffocate inside my stuffy house, I bundled my children into snowsuits and jackets and took them out into the cold. Their cheeks turned scarlet and their noses ran, but we were glad to feel the air against our faces. My daughter played on the swing, singing to herself as her hair blew out behind her. And my son, who was a few months past two at the time, sat on the back step, his eyes fixed on the trees tossing in the wind. He wore an expression of both terror and delight. "They're waving at me," he said at last.

Living with my young children, I had the chance to experience a different way of looking at the world. Isolated from other adults, immersed in my children's reality, I found myself rediscovering a worldview I had long forgotten. It had lain buried beneath the rational empiricism of years of education—but that day, sitting beside my son on the back step, I looked at the trees' windblown branches and I found myself thinking: Maybe they *are* waving. I knew it was the wind that moved them, of course, but it seemed to me that the branches were not lifeless things pushed back and forth by moving air. Instead, the wind animated the trees. It rushed through the trees and against our faces like some great, wild Being. And as it blew, both the trees and I were quickened by its force. My son grabbed my hand, and we leapt and danced across the lawn.

Wind is the first metaphor the Old Testament uses for God. Genesis 1:1–2 says,

> At the beginning of God's creating of the heavens and the
> earth,
> when the earth was wild and waste,
> darkness over the face of Ocean,

rushing-spirit of God hovering over the face of the waters....
(Schocken Bible)

The word for "rushing-spirit" is *ruah,* a Hebrew word translated throughout the Old and New Testaments as both "spirit" and "wind." For the same concept, the Greeks used *pneuma,* which can mean spirit...wind...breath. These ancient cultures saw breath and spirit as intertwined concepts; both were the energy that flows from being, the expression of living essence. Thus, the Holy Spirit is the breath of God, the expression of all God is. The wind, like divinity, is both powerful and invisible. No boundary line can block the force of its expression, and wind gusts into wind, a dynamic fusion of energy.

Jesus said of the Spirit:

The wind blows wherever it pleases. You hear its sound but
you cannot tell where it comes from or where it is going.
So it is with everyone born of the Spirit. (John 3:8)

God's Spirit blows through creation, animating us all with life; the universe's life force is intimately bound together with the Force of God. In Genesis 2:1, when Yahweh had formed the human from the dust of the soil, he blew into the nostrils, "the breath of life and the human became a living being" (Schocken Bible). Is it possible the divine wind still animates us all?

We feel most alive when we are inspired to act, to create, to love and hold one another, to change the world for the better. Through no coincidence, the concept of inspiration comes from the same linguistic root as the word *spirit,* and the Old and New Testaments clearly make the connection. According to 2 Timothy 3:16, work that is inspired is "God-breathed."

In other words, our creativity is both the expression of our deepest essence—and the expression of God's essence. It is God who breathes our individual essence through each one of us; it is God who stirs this essence with the wind of his Spirit: It is God who inspires us.

According to Meister Eckhart, "All creatures want to express God in all their works." Matthew Fox, commenting on Eckhart, writes, "The flowing out that creation is about is also a flowing back, a return. The exit is a return; the return an exit." This flowing out and hurrying back is the rhythm of the divine breath animating creation—and ourselves. Human creativity is God's breath merging with our own.

But how does this work out in our everyday lives?

In my own life, my days no longer feel as confined and airless as they once did. My children are all in school now, and I have uninterrupted hours each day to devote to my work. But my life is still a hodgepodge of responsibilities. I feel a desperate need to sort out the demands of family, finances, home, career, art, self—and God. I am too busy to feel inspired, too overwhelmed to feel any sense of divine wind rushing through my life.

The laws of perspective and geometry long ago infiltrated my mind, telling me two things cannot be in the same space at the same time: My chair cannot occupy the area of another object; the wind is simply moving air that does not penetrate my skin's boundary lines; and somehow I must find individual pigeonholes in my life for all the conflicting demands of my many roles. When I can't, I simply answer the loudest call and leave the rest neglected. I imagine my childhood self looking at me with scorn and pity: I'm such a grown-up lately, worried about bills and cleaning the house and meeting deadlines. Dancing in the wind seems like a waste of time.

But Christ said that the kingdom of God belongs to those who are like children—and a child's world is full of overlapping realities. My younger children are quite comfortable with my chair filling the same space as a snug home for fairies. And they're equally at home with the idea that the wind is both moving air *and* the loving female image of God they find in George MacDonald's fantasy, *At the Back of the North Wind*.

Some moments bring to us a sharp awareness of the wind of God blowing through our lives. But does he breathe silently and surely through even our most hassled days? Invisible, forgotten, unfazed, can he somehow occupy the same space as our own frantic egos? Or is reality a narrow, empirical thing after all?

Rushing to keep up with our busy schedules, most of us like to keep our feet on the ground. We don't have time for flights of fancy; we don't even have time for the serendipitous stirring of grace. But a nagging little wind may whistle through the tiny gaps in our well-planned lives, like a cold draft on our necks, reminding us that something is wrong. Sooner or later, that chilly draft will grow to gale force. When it does, we will have no choice but to reconsider the way we live our lives.

The wind of God is not always a warm, gentle breeze. Sometimes it's a cold, fierce blast that buffets away all our comfortable preconceptions. The process is often far from pleasant. But like a kite tangled in the wires, we need to be freed from all that holds us earthbound. Only then will we be able to fly.

For earlier cultures, like the Celts, wonder and meaning breathed through the tangible world. Greek philosophy, however, began the separation of spirit and body that Western science later continued. As heirs to this thinking, we subtract mystery and spirit from the physical world, leaving the spirit floating like an intangible dream, while matter becomes heavy and inanimate.

But Einstein's theory of relativity began the process of pushing back the rigid frontiers of Western empiricism. According to this new thinking, reality is a startling, unlikely thing, as filled with paradox as the kingdom of God. Things are not what they seem, this new science tells us. Physical reality lacks the hard outlines we assumed it had, and the universe is mysteriously connected and conscious.

Do we dare step outside our mental boundaries into this rushing realm of new ideas? If we have the courage to see with children's eyes again, will we find joy and terror, wonder and life blowing toward us from the world's four corners? According to theologian A. W. Tozer, the breath of God fills the world with "living potentiality."

But the word *Spirit* lacks any tangible shape. It's a hazy mysterious word, a concept the imagination finds difficult to grasp. If we push the metaphor still further, however, we find a more familiar face. The wind is a metaphor for God's expression of himself, and if Christ is the Word of God—God's self-expression—then Christ too is the breath that animates the universe. Conceptually, the Spirit is alive and moving, but Christ goes further; he stretches out to us scarred, human hands. This makes the metaphor more personal, more insistent—and more difficult. Rational thinking tells us no human being can animate the entire universe. Can we find the courage to feel Jesus of Nazareth breathing through us, through the world? Or is this thought merely a comforting fantasy?

The Christian Celts, however, believed Christ animated even the most ordinary aspects of the physical world; everyday reality expressed his love and presence steadily and intimately. Their prayers speak of "Christ beside me, Christ before me; Christ behind me, Christ within me; Christ beneath me, Christ above me."

This view of Christianity lures me; I long to find Christ in the ordinary sequence of my daily life. But too much of my existence is lived far from the simple patterns of nature, and Christ does not seem obviously present in the hum of the fax machine and the dishwasher, the nagging insistence of voice mail and my oven buzzer. I look at the Celts' daily work through the romantic haze cast by distance, and my heart aches for their simpler world.

My life does not ask me to tend a fire or care for cattle, knead bread or scrub the kitchen floor on my knees—and so I forget that this was hard, physical labor. If the Celtic Christians could feel Christ's wind in their faces while they worked from dawn till night at these ordinary menial tasks, then maybe I too can pause to feel the breeze that stirs the dust on my furniture, ruffles the stacks of paper on my desk, and whips our wet laundry dry.

All summer the outdoor air blows through our open windows, filling the house with the fragrance of grass and rain. As fall draws nearer, the air grows sharp, but I hate to give in and close the windows. My children shivered in their pajamas while they ate their cereal this morning, but I am glad we can still smell the sweet, clean wind. And even in the winter, when the windows are shut tight, our house will not be a total vacuum. The cold gales will gust around our house, and air will find its way through open doors and tiny cracks, bringing fresh oxygen to our wintry lungs.

Today I will write another chapter; I will wipe the table and sweep the kitchen floor, pick up the clutter from the living room, and throw two loads of laundry into the machine; I will pack lunches and make supper; I will pay bills and return phone calls; and I will supervise my children's chores and homework, laugh with them and hug them tight, then read to them and pray with them before they sleep. But if I stop still and listen, maybe in the midst of all this I will hear the breeze that whispers through our open windows. And like an echo, I will heave a sigh of relief.

The wind blows where it wills. Every day is Pentecost.

If you ask me how I believe in God, how God creates Himself in me, and reveals Himself to me, my answer may provoke your smiles or laughter, and even scandalize you. I believe in God as I believe in my friends, because I feel the breath of His affection....

—MIGUEL DE UNAMUNO

"Everything, dreaming and all, has got a soul in it...."
So saying, North Wind lifted Diamond and bore him away.

—GEORGE MACDONALD,
AT THE BACK OF THE NORTH WIND

Bow daily before God and wait for breathings to you from his Spirit.

—ISAAC PENNINGTON

3

Water

Ho, every one that thirsteth, come ye to the waters....

—ISAIAH 55:1 KJV

You...are a deep sea:
The more I enter you, the more I discover,
and the more I discover, the more I seek you.

—CATHERINE OF SIENA

I have a recurring dream about the ocean. Usually, I'm walking a long distance, trying to reach it. In the end, when I finally arrive at the shore, I am filled with a deep sense of achievement and rightness. That quickly changes to dread, however, as without warning the waves rise higher before me. Unable to move, I watch them eat away the dry land; eventually, I too am swept away. In my dream, I am both afraid and exhilarated. I know I am likely to drown. But I don't. I am overpowered but unharmed, swept out to sea alive.

So what does the ocean represent in my dreams? Life? Or death? Or God himself, as mysterious and dangerous, as fertile and lovely as the sea?

Raised in an evangelical church, my mind is saturated with water metaphors for God. The Bible, particularly the Psalms, uses the metaphor again and again:

As the hart panteth after the water brooks, so panteth my soul after thee, O God. (Ps 42:1 KJV)

17

O God, thou art my God; early will I seek thee: my soul thirsteth for thee, my flesh longeth for thee in a dry and thirsty land, where no water is. (Ps 63:1 KJV)

He shall come down like rain upon the mown grass: as showers that water the earth. (Ps 72:6 KJV)

Water is essential to our physical bodies and to the physical environment in which we live. Which leads to a simple proof I remember from tenth-grade geometry class: If $a = b$, and $b = c$, then $a = c$. God, says the psalmist, equals water. Water equals life. Then, it follows, God equals life (that which sustains us, nourishes us, helps us to grow).

The metaphor fills me with surprised delight, for I've encountered other metaphors for God that are as dry as dust. These images of God threaten to constrict me rather than help me grow; they destroy rather than create. God, according to this way of thinking, is a cold, sterile Being who keeps himself rigidly separate from life's muddy waters. This Being seeks to deny me rather than multiply me. He hides himself in out-of-the-way corners that are difficult to reach; he withholds himself from the entirety of my life, confining himself to arid moments of sacrifice and effort.

Water, on the other hand, permeates everything. It defies boundaries. It seeps in through the smallest cracks in my heart, it makes life, green and varied and spreading, spring up within me. It is life itself.

Having said that, some part of me wants to shake its head in disapproval. No, it says, you're implying that God is an easy, feel-good sort of Being, a God with low expectations, a vague, psychedelic sort of God that slops around the universe, as accessible as water. But I didn't pick the image, after all. Jesus himself implied that he is the living water (John 4:10–13). And John, the author of the Book of Revelations, wrote:

Whoever is thirsty, let him come; and whoever wishes, let him take the free gift of the water of life. (22:17)

But because this water is free and life-giving doesn't mean that it is not also dangerous. Water in the natural world is often beyond our ability to control. It gives life—but it can be destructive. This untamed and unknowable quality is what frightens me in my dream. If the ocean sweeps over me, then I will no longer be in control of my own life. If the waves eat away my selfish ego, what will be left? The ocean's waters can be terrifying.

Last spring, walking by the ocean, I was suddenly struck by how much death had washed up on the shore: rotting fish; the drowned body of a seagull; the clean, bleached bones of some small animal. Death is the dark side of water's metaphor. Creation and destruction flow together. But what does that have to do with the image of God?

Behind almost any symbol's light lies a shadow, like the dark side of the moon. Focusing on the lit area can be useful, but what do we do with the uncomfortable shadowy part? Do we simply ignore it? Maybe it's ultimately irrelevant; after all, a metaphor is not meant to be literal truth.

Our culture doesn't like to think of death. I certainly don't. Like most people, I prefer to push it out of my thoughts. Busy with my career and my family, I had pushed death into one of the untidy mental closets I never opened. If the door ever cracked ajar, I pushed it shut again with thoughts of an upcoming work project or my family's next birthday party. Death was irrelevant to my life.

Meanwhile, God flickered through my busy life, like a faraway glimpse of water between the trees. I thirsted for him some days, sought him halfheartedly, took sips of his life in the small pauses in my life's busy pace—but I feared him too. To come face to face with God might also mean taking another look at death. Eternity, after all, is as wide and fathomless as the sea; I preferred my landlocked life, full of the familiar demands I could control. I felt powerful, aware of my own strength, glad to inhabit my life.

But sometimes we run into events that slam against us like cold, dark tidal waves, knocking us off our feet, wiping away the familiar landscapes of our lives. When that happens, we face the truth we've tried to hide: Everything dies. Life, no matter how wet and green, hides a skull. And the sea, the water that covers so much of the earth, can give life—and it can also bring death. It teems with creatures—and it is as empty as any desert.

Last spring, when we came home from our vacation at the ocean, we found that the creek down the road from our house had flooded its banks. The water had swept away small trees and tangled undergrowth, leaving only a sodden plain of brown silt. And sooner or later, I've been forced to accept, death sweeps over life, bringing the destruction of all that is established and familiar.

⌘

But today the same creek seems as safe as a well-loved friend. I sit here with my notebook on my knees, my feet in the warm water. The creek is brown with algae, but the reflections of fern and sumac, sycamores and travelers' joy lie in green and white ripples over the dark water. My children bring me buckets of silvery minnows and crayfish like baby lobsters, flat-footed snails and strings of moss-green algae. My oldest laughs and splashes like my seven-year-old, then suddenly takes herself thirty feet away and curls on a rock, her hair streaming down her back in a long, dripping hank of mermaid curls. The younger two go upstream, and after a few moments, my oldest joins them. Together they move to the deepest part of the creek, where the water runs slow and cold.

I hear their voices coming back to me on the summer air. They're pretending they are mer-people who have swum too near to humans and have forgotten their true identities. Years have passed while they lived out entire lifetimes on land. Now, splashing in the water, they say they catch glimpses of another life, memories of their lost watery home.

Listening to their voices mixed with the creek's constant murmur, death seems far away. The water at my feet is dappled with sunlight and striped with minnows; everywhere I look, I see life crawling and creeping and wriggling. Beside me, the banks are no longer

21

brown and covered with silt. Instead, the fertile mud has yielded a lush tangle of tall grass, Queen Anne's lace, and purple loosestrife. And the water's never-ending voice speaks to me of eternity hidden at the center of everything, flowing in a ceaseless stream through both life and death.

Like my children's imaginary mer-people, I often forget my true identity. I wander through my earthbound life, unaware that I was born with the ability to breathe even in the coldest deepest depths. I keep my mental rooms neat and dry and tidy, with all the messy forgotten fears and fancies shoved out of sight.

But just now, listening to my children's voices and the sound of water, I caught a glimpse of another life, a life that's unlimited and forever. And inside my mind, God's grace seeped under the tight-shut doors and trickled through my thoughts, bringing life.

<hr/>

We often lack the courage to venture out past the warm shallow water that holds no shadows. That's why we keep our metaphors safe and small.

But imagine yourself on an ocean beach, playing in the waves. At first, you keep close to the shore, where the water is flat and white with froth. Gradually, though, you go a little farther out, and then a little farther....Almost before you realize it, enormous waves are tossing around you. Each time a glassy-green mountain comes surging toward you, you are filled with terror. This time you will be smashed, drowned....

And then the wave hits you. You let go, abandoning your control of your body—and find that instead of pushing you under, the wave lifts you up. That moment when your weight is borne by the water leaves you laughing and breathless, almost intoxicated with joy.

Death will dissolve neither God's image nor our own.

Water

In the glory of His wisdom, this river of grace gave joy to God....
That is why you should please Him by doing that which gives Him
the most joy: come to the waters, dive into them, and do not be
afraid of drowning. Trust God alone as you float in His grace,
borne by the current into His paradise....

—JOHN BUNYAN

This last water which we have described is so abundant that,
were it not that the ground is incapable of receiving it, we might
believe this cloud of great Majesty to be here on this earth....

What will it be, then, when the soul is completely
engulfed in such water?

—TERESA OF AVILA

4

Darkness

The day of the Lord cometh, for it is nigh at hand;
A day of darkness and of gloominess, a day of clouds
and of thick darkness.

—JOEL 2:1–2 KJV

Clouds and darkness are round about him.

—PSALM 97:2 KJV

Late one Friday, under cover of the night, my daughter Emily's hamster escaped from its cage. With a wail of loss and terror, she discovered he was gone the next morning. Her door had been shut all night, so we were fairly sure he couldn't have gone far. We searched through all her room's dark corners, beneath the bed, inside her closet, but we could not find the little animal. When I pulled a pile of paper dolls and school papers out from under her chest of drawers, I caught a glimpse of the heat vent, and my heart sank.

Our vents are the old-fashioned kind, set in the wall just above the floor, covered with a metal grid; the holes are just hamster-sized. When we had searched everywhere in her room, I was certain of the truth: The hamster had fallen down the heat vent.

Emily went through the next day with a pale, tear-stained face. She refused to sleep in her room and instead curled up at night on the pantry floor, comforted by the refrigerator's hum. Her room was stained with death now, and she entered it only to get her clothes. I dreaded the day when the summer's heat would bring the smell of decay rising from the vent.

"It was just a rodent," my husband said. "These thing happen."
I knew he was right. A hamster's life span is not all that long under
the best of conditions; I hadn't even been particularly attached to the
animal. But I felt as though death's shadow had fallen across our
home. I resented that Emily had to catch a whiff of its dark odor.

At first glance, darkness does not seem to be a viable metaphor
for God. We tend to equate darkness with pain and confusion, and
ultimately with death. Our memories of old hurts, our anxieties for
the future, these hold nothing that seems productive or worthwhile.
Instead, they seem chaotic, dysfunctional, and...well, *dark*. If we live
in darkness, we can't see clearly: not ourselves, not others, not God.
Darkness feels like God's absence.

But as an adolescent, I loved the dark. Whenever I was upset, I
would climb at night out my bedroom window and sit on the roof,
feeling safe and comforted by the soft darkness that wrapped around
me. I sought opportunities to be outside at night.

When I went camping with my friend Joyce, we would lie
unafraid in the black woods, unseen life and mystery pressing in
around our sleeping bags. Side by side on our backs, we would talk
about boys and our parents and God. She was more skeptical about
Christianity than I; I felt a need to defend the Bible against her cyni-
cism. "Our pastor says in heaven there will be no more night," she said
once, her voice filled with scorn. "Who would want to miss this?" She
waved her hand up against the night sky.

I felt there was something wrong with her argument, but unable
to find a legitimate answer, I resorted to a lie. "The Bible says somewhere—I think in Job—that God is a dazzling darkness. Like this." I
too waved my hand at the dark.

Since I was a minister's daughter, we both tacitly acknowledged I
had the final word when it came to the Scriptures. "That's cool," Joyce
said mildly, and we fell silent. I heard her breathing even out into sleep,

while I stared into the darkness, feeling a tinge of guilt over my lie. But if the Bible didn't say the words I had told her, I reasoned, it ought to.

More than twenty years later, I was surprised to run across echoes of my fabricated "dazzling darkness" in the writings of both Pseudo-Dionysius and Saint Bonaventure. They speak of God as "brilliant darkness," "superluminous darkness," "a darkness in which everything is super-resplendent and in which everything shines out." Saint Bonaventure quotes Exodus 33:20, "No one may see me and live" (NLT), and concludes,

> Let us, then, die
> and enter into the darkness;
> let us impose silence
> upon our cares, our desires and our imaginings.

Though I had not yet read these Christian mystics, through my teenage years and into young adulthood I was comforted by this divine image of rest and silence. When life was difficult, I craved the night. Darkness gave me restoration, inspiration, a sense of God's presence. Although I had not read John of the Cross either, if I had, I would have responded to his words.

> One dark night
> . . .
> I went out unseen,
> My house being now all stilled;
>
> In darkness, and secure,
> By the secret ladder disguised,
> —Ah, the sheer grace!—
> In the darkness and concealment,
> My house being now all stilled;
>
> On that glad night,
> In secret, for no one saw me

27

> Nor did I look at anything,
> With no other light or guide
> Than the one that burned in my heart;
>
> This guided me
> More securely than the light of noon
> To where he waited for me
> —Him I knew so well—
> In a place where no one else appeared.

Back then my understanding of these words might have been shallow, but I would have been sure I knew how to climb that secret ladder into God's night.

Today, I'm not so certain. When the mystics spoke of God as a silent, glimmering darkness, I suspect they were trying to reach past the sensual metaphors; they were standing on verbal tiptoes, straining to describe an experience of God that was unlimited by human images. They were attempting to do without divine metaphors.

Ultimately, they failed, of course. Darkness may be an image without shape, without scent or sound—yet it is still a metaphor, a construct of our intellectual capacity for forming analogies. But this metaphor describes an experience that few of us find comfortable: the loss of control.

In the dark, we cannot see what lies ahead. If we dare to walk at all, then we walk blindly, trusting ourselves to the darkness itself, despite the knowledge that the night may hide danger. We cannot chart our future course; we may not even be able to recognize where we have come from. We have no choice but to surrender our control of our own lives.

No wonder then that we equate darkness and death, for death is the ultimate loss of control. We cannot predict what comes next—if anything. When we are forced to personally confront this darkness, we do so with anxiety, if not terror: Since we cannot anticipate and control the events in our lives, surely these events will harm us. Our discomfort with both darkness and death is rooted in paranoia.

When we speak of "dark times" in our lives, we generally mean moments of anguish and confusion and failure. We cannot see how God could hide himself in the midst of such pain. No divine clarity glimmers in our bewilderment, and so we tend to revert to the common equation: Darkness equals evil equals death equals terror. God is light, and the dark only hides his face. We crave order, a sense of control—but we are powerless against the black events that threaten to destroy our lives.

Lying awake earlier this summer, I counted money instead of sheep. Again and again, I tallied up the checks I could anticipate; then I would subtract the upcoming bills. The final answer to my arithmetic might give me a moment of relief, until I remembered I had forgotten to subtract some essential and substantial expense. I would begin my mental math all over again; this time the answer would fill me with anxiety. But no, I had forgotten a check we expected next month....As I lay there obsessed by my calculations, I would hear a *squeak-squeak-squeak* from down the hall. In my daughter's dark room, her hamster would be running on its wheel. And with the same senseless frenzy, I would scurry through my addition and subtraction yet again.

"What are the first two words that come to your mind when you think of money?" a friend asked me when I told her about my nightly obsession.

"Safety." I answered before I could rationalize the logic of my answer. "Control."

She nodded, her eyebrows raised, leaving me to draw my own conclusions. I'd been trying to raise a wall of dollars against the darkness in my life. It was a flimsy, useless structure, of course. If you shut yourself in a box to keep out the dark, it's darker yet inside your box.

"When you sit in the darkness long enough," another friend told me, "eventually you begin to see. Stop fighting the darkness. Make friends with it."

But most of us don't like to be friends with darkness. Through sheer will power, we'd rather press the shadows out of our lives. We may accept that all of us must face our quota of dark times, but we'd like to keep that quota manageable, something small enough that we can tuck it away in an out-of-the-way corner of our lives. When we are unable to grasp the dark and wrench it into the compact, tidy shape we want it to take, we are filled with frustration and despair.

The unknown author of *The Cloud of Unknowing* speaks often of darkness as a metaphor for God, but the author's term does not refer to the ordinary confusion and troubles we all inevitably face. What he describes in paragraphs like this one is something much more lofty and spiritual:

> You will seem to know nothing and to feel nothing except a naked intent toward God in the depths of your being. Try as you might, this darkness and this cloud will remain between you and your God. You will feel frustrated, for your mind will be unable to grasp him, and your heart will not relish the delight of his love. But learn to be at home in this darkness. Return to it as often as you can, letting your spirit cry out to him you love. For if, in this life, you hope to feel and see God as he is in himself it must be within this darkness and this cloud.

This is a mystical experience, and the pain and frustration the author mentions are beyond the ordinary human pain we all experience. Spiritual "unknowing" is encountered on a far higher plane than most of us ever attain.

Or do we simply not recognize the true significance of "dark times"? Financial troubles, the loss of relationships, professional frustrations, physical and emotional pain of one sort or another—all these steal from us our sense of personal control. They demand that we walk forward into the future without knowing where we are going. We have no choice but to abandon ourselves to something unknown, some force beyond ourselves.

We seldom recognize this as a positive experience. I certainly don't. And yet in *Motherhood: A Spiritual Journey,* I affirmed that

> Life comes out of darkness. Look at the seed that lies in the ground before it can grow. Look at our own babies who grew in the shadowy interiors of our bodies before they were born into the light. Out of the darkness, God creates new life. Even in the shadows, he is with us.

The presence of God is sometimes most tangible when we have totally lost control of our own lives.

But even if we accept that darkness is fertile and life-giving, mysteriously infused with God's presence, can we take the next step and say that the dark is not only *filled with* God but it *is* God himself? Surely the metaphor asks too much of our imaginations. The Bible speaks of light and day as metaphors for God, while darkness is generally equated with separation from him. Loss and illness and death are undeniably evil; how can we hope to touch God in the midst of anguished nights?

And yet I remember the joy I once felt lying in the darkness. I had no adult agenda then, no schedule that required bright lights and careful control, no grown-up anxieties to nag at me. Instead, I could simply relax, trusting the darkness with a weightless sense of confidence and freedom. The touch of the night sky against my face was like a kiss.

Light is a wonderful metaphor for God, but no image, even such a bright one, can contain him. In the Old Testament Book of Exodus, God descends on Mount Sinai as fire and light—and as a dark cloud. Deuteronomy describes the mountain as "shrouded in black clouds and deep darkness"; in Exodus 20:21, "Moses entered into the deep darkness where God was" (NLT). The psalmist too found this metaphor a useful one; in Psalm 18 he writes that "darkness was under God's feet" and "he made darkness his secret place" (KJV). Like the mystics, the ancient biblical saints experienced God in those fearful moments when they were forced to abandon their intellect and senses—all their human abilities to exercise control over their lives—and simply trust.

In the dark, we cannot see the next step ahead of us. We cannot even see if there is solid ground ahead at all. Do we dare to stop scrabbling for something solid to hold onto—and simply let ourselves drop?

On Sunday, the third day after the hamster's disappearance, I shuffled around the kitchen making coffee, wondering when the dead animal would begin to smell and what we would say to our daughter.

As I sat down to drink my coffee, I vaguely missed our cat's presence. Every morning she twines between my feet, purring at my company and the promise of food, but I hadn't seen her yet this morning. With a sinking in my heart, I wondered if she had somehow found the hamster's body. She loves to carry an old rabbit's foot around in her mouth, and I could imagine how fascinated she would be with a limp, furry hamster corpse. Emily was still in the shower, and I got to my feet, prepared to deal quickly with whatever needed to be dealt with.

When I called the cat's name, I heard an answering meow from the basement. I went down the stairs, peering into the shadows.

She was crouched in the corner by the furnace. Seeing me, she chirped and pattered toward me, then ran back to the furnace. Her paws up on the metal side, she looked over her shoulder at me. She gave another insistent mew. When I turned to go back upstairs, she refused to leave her post beside the furnace.

I ran to get my husband, and together we took off one gray panel from the furnace's side. "No hamster could have survived a drop from the second floor," my husband muttered. The panel yawed forward with a creak, and we shone a flashlight inside.

A tiny furry nose poked out at us.

I shrieked and grabbed the cat. Like Mary who ran to tell the disciples about the empty grave, I raced up the stairs to the bathroom. "He's alive! We found him!"

Naked and sputtering, Emily grabbed a towel and tumbled down the basement stairs. I watched as she bent over and groped through the darkness. I couldn't see her face—the corner by the furnace was too full of shadows—but when she scooped the hamster up into her hands, I was dazzled by her joy.

After we brought the hamster upstairs, we found that sometime during his ordeal, he lost an eye. He seemed unfazed by his injury, and the empty socket healed without complications. I visit him regularly these days. Before his adventure, he would disappear inside his house if I approached and scold me if I came too near. Now, when I lift the cover off the cage, he runs into my hand with a new trust that surprises me. When I hold him, his one bright eye looks up at me, and he vibrates with energy and curiosity.

Still, he is just a rodent. In another year or two at most, he will go the way of all flesh. And yet for my daughter and me, his story is as full of promise as the Gospels' parables, those long extended metaphors told by Jesus.

⸺⸺⸺

Do we find the divine presence *in spite of* the dark? Or is the darkness itself somehow divine?

We're accustomed to thinking of God in terms of light and order. But in the beginning, in the primeval chaos, the Book of Genesis claims that "darkness was upon the face of the deep," and it equates this darkness with God's Spirit. Before light, before order, before creation even, God's presence *is* the dark. And between Good Friday and the resurrection, when Jesus lay dead in the dark tomb, the Book of First Peter claims Christ's presence somehow "preached unto the spirits in prison."

Still, darkness is not an easy metaphor for God, or a comforting one. The hamster fell into the dark and lost an eye; and when Jacob wrestled all night with a nameless stranger, his leg was disjointed and he limped away when morning came. If we too step into the dark, we cannot hope to escape unscathed.

As we fall, we can only trust we drop into God's hands.

Thus out of this night springs first the knowledge of oneself, and on that, as a foundation, is built up the knowledge of God.

—JOHN OF THE CROSS

This clear darkness of God is the purity of heart Christ spoke of....

—THOMAS MERTON

By an undivided and absolute abandonment of yourself and everything, shedding all and freed from all, you will be uplifted to the ray of the divine shadow which is above everything else.

—PSEUDO-DIONYSIUS

5

Fire and Light

You are a fire always burning but never consuming;
you are a fire consuming in your heart all the soul's selfish love;
you are a fire lifting all chill and giving light.
You are that light beyond light.

—CATHERINE OF SIENA

I am the light of the world;
he that followeth me...shall have the light of life.

—JESUS OF NAZARETH (JOHN 8:12 KJV)

If we are seeing persons, we take the presence of light in our lives for granted—but light is a very odd thing. Light's presence in our lives is such a constant given, we forget our entire existence is oriented on it as a precondition. Without light, we could not read or write (without learning a new tactile language); we could not drive a car; we could not judge our friends' feelings by the lines of their bodies and the expressions on their faces. We would have to find entire new ways to orientate ourselves in relation to physical reality. And yet we cannot measure light's shape nor define it chemically; we may be able to feel a fire's heat, but we cannot touch its light with any sense except our eyes.

Toward the end of the nineteenth century, a lonely boy began to think about light. He was a small, strange misfit who did not do well in school; perhaps he was too busy wondering about the properties of light to master arithmetic. His parents must have worried about him. After all, few six-year-olds are obsessed with something so abstract.

The question that fascinated him most was this: What would a beam of light look like if he could catch up with it? If he could run fast enough to race alongside a sunbeam, what would he see?

I can imagine his mother sighing to herself whenever he asked the question. It's the same sort of silly, no-answer query my son is forever asking me. Sometimes, I'll stop what I'm doing, delighted by the quirkiness of his thinking, but other times, when I'm concentrating on my own adult thoughts, I answer absently, impatiently. I wonder if Einstein's mother was a patient woman.

Einstein found his own answers to his question. He decided if he could go the speed of light, he would see something totally different than what we usually think of as light. If he were freed from plodding time and human limitations, he surmised, he would see light as something eternal and motionless, a series of frozen waves.

He continued thinking about light for the next ten years, and by the time he was sixteen he had learned enough mathematics to decide his conclusion had been wrong. Instead, he began to believe something even more nonsensical: No matter how fast you go, light will always travel at the same speed ahead of you.

This is very strange stuff. And it gets still stranger the further you go. After thinking about light for decade after decade, Einstein reached even more startling conclusions. Our brains perceive only three spatial dimensions, but Einstein proved mathematically that the behavior of light can only be explained by the existence of more dimensions. Theodr Kaluza, a mathematician who took Einstein's theories still further, determined that mathematically light and gravity are very similar things.

This makes no sense of course, at least not to me. But I can't help but wonder if an organism exists that can "see" gravity the way I see light. At any rate, Kaluza concluded that light, like gravity, is a warp, a vibration, a sort of crumple in a dimension beyond our own.

I think of the minnows that dart around our feet when my children and I wade in the creek. How do their eyes perceive our shapes above the water? Can they hear our voices? We must seem to them like vague vibrations from another world, a world they are physiologically incapable of experiencing. In the same way, is light the flickering shadow of some motion in another dimension, a dimension I cannot even imagine because of my own biological limitations?

"Life itself," wrote Sir Thomas Browne, "is but the shadow of eternity...and light but the shadow of God."

Fire and light are perhaps the most common metaphors for divinity. Poets and theologians and mystics have referred to God as light since long before Christ.

The Greek word *phos* meant sunlight, fire, eyesight—and it also meant salvation and life. When Plato wrote *The Republic,* he forever linked in Western minds "the good" and "the light." Today, we've nearly forgotten the presence of a metaphor; instead, we often see goodness and light as synonyms.

The Hebrew Old Testament puts a slightly different twist on the concept. Genesis describes light as God's firstborn, that which was created before all else. Stars do not create light because they burn; instead, they bear light as though it were a child, a precious gift they deliver to the world. They are vehicles for some still greater power than themselves.

Throughout the Old Testament, fire and light indicate God's nearness. The torch of his presence led the Israelites through the desert (Exod 13:21), and the psalmist claims the divine light as his salvation (Ps 27:1). The Old Testament authors distinguish between God's actual being, however, and his self-manifestation. Light, they say, is God's garment (Ps 104:2); light dwells with God (Dan 2:22); his presence is accompanied by light (Exod 19:12). In the New Testament, the disciples saw Jesus "shine as the sun, and his raiment was white as the light" (Matt 17:2 KJV), and in the Book of Revelation, Christ has eyes like flame (1:15; 2:18).

John the Evangelist carries the metaphor another step. Light is not only the manifestation of divine presence; Jesus, John wrote, *is* light, "the true Light, who gives light to everyone" (John 1:9 NLT). The light of which John speaks is life itself, a light that will never be overcome (John 1:4–5). Christ is that which allows us to "see"—to orientate ourselves in relation to all other things. He has come as "light into the world" (John 12:46).

And yet, in all honesty, I have to confess I find light to be a daunting metaphor for God. Fire was the Greek god Prometheus's gift to humanity, and fire and light are life-giving, yes—but too much of either one is destructive. Like Saint Paul on the road to Damascus, the direct rays of the divine presence may burn our vision; in the end, the fire may consume us altogether, leaving only cinders behind. The metaphor is too intense, as vehement and fierce as summer lightning.

Still, while we may not always be comfortable with a God of fire and light, our minds have been stamped with the concept that light equals goodness, while darkness equals evil. When we can't escape this centuries-old mental rut, we end up with a dualistic universe, a black-and-white world where light opposes dark. And like the Greeks, like the Gnostics, like the church itself in ages past, we extend the equation: Light equals goodness equals spirit—and dark equals evil equals the body.

At some level, we end up believing that our physical selves are sinful, separated from God's light. But though our bodies are too frail to withstand a blazing God, still, they are the identities we know best. Most of us lack the unflinching passion of the mystics; we are reluctant to offer our physical selves as fuel for the divine fire. But a dualistic view of reality leaves us with a concept of spirit too watery and flimsy to comfort us for the loss of our more familiar and solid selves.

Perhaps, after all, we'd be more comfortable if we stuck with darkness as a metaphor for God. Darkness does not have to be terrifying; it can be as gentle and nurturing as the womb. A deity like this would not blaze and sear but instead would wrap us in comforting arms.

Even if we choose darkness as the better metaphor, though, we are still condemned to a monochromatic image of the world. We are turning our backs on the world of color.

Dr. Rudolfo Llinas, a neuroscientist at New York University, dismisses light as "nothing but electromagnetic radiation. Colors," he adds, "clearly don't exist outside our brains." Well, obviously, for those of us who lack the mathematical genius of Einstein or Kaluza, our ideas about light are shaped by the characteristics of the sense organ we use to perceive it. Our eyes are capable of seeing color only when light is refracted, when it is broken into "pieces" the cones of our retinas distinguish as separate qualities. Color is really light. And whether we trust the mathematicians or the mystics, apparently light is something "real."

As I leap from metaphor to metaphor, I find color—broken light—to be a better stepping-stone toward God. The glare of intense fire is too bright for my eyes, but colors are full of life and nuance. The church has made of color a metaphor in itself, using red and blue, purple and white to symbolize the different aspects of our life in Christ—he who is passionate and pure, royal and ever living.

A God of color is not limited by a dualistic image of the universe, where everything is either black or white, flesh or spirit. Instead, Christ, the God who became body and then died (as light is shattered into colors), is full of infinite richness and startling variety. He is the purple and gold of autumn asters growing beside the road; he is shades of brown and pink, like human flesh; he is the soft dim blue of the early morning sky; he is the splash of red graffiti on a city wall.

We fear a God of pure white flame, because he seems to say no to so much that is important to us. But according to author and theologian G. K. Chesterton,

> White...is not a mere absence of colour; it is a shining and affirmative thing, as fierce as red, as definite as black.... God paints in many colours; but He never paints so gorgeously, I almost said so gaudily, as when He paints in white.

A God of pure light does not lack color; he does not say no to everything but whiteness, for all the colors of the universe dance and flicker
within his flame. He says yes to vermilion and indigo, burnt umber
and cerise, magenta and ocher: all the burning hues and softest pas-
tels, the concrete shades and nuances of our world.

It might be easier to live like moles, making tiny tunnels without the
help of vision, eyes screwed tight against the sun's glare. Why should
we allow light, this shadow from another world, into our lives? We
might do quite well without light's eternal question mark prodding us
toward the chaotic, startling world of quantum physics. After all,
Newton's orderly universe was far more tangible and rational. We
don't need our lives shaken by the vibrations of something unknown
and unknowable.

But then imagine yourself as a mountain shepherd, your brain
scoured empty by sand and rock and loneliness. As you climb behind
your sheep, you hear the thin song of the wind through the dry grass,
and the high, keening cry of a hawk far above your head in the blazing blue sky. You breathe in the odors of sheep dung and dry earth,
and all of these scents and sights and sounds are the same as they have
been for countless days before.

Gradually, though, you become aware of something different,
something that does not belong. A leap of light catches at the corner
of your vision. Curious, you turn aside from your path.

A small tree is burning. The heat from the flames makes the sky
ripple, but the fire is oddly silent. You take a slow step closer, and still
you do not hear the crackle of wood and leaf being eaten by fire. You
neither see nor smell smoke; there is only the bright blue and gold
flow of flame over the gnarled branches and dark green leaves.

You stand staring. And then, despite the hot dry air, a chill line
of goose bumps rises along your arms: The bush burns but is not consumed. Flame leaps from every twig, and yet the tree is not dimin-
ished; it remains itself, whole and intact.

What does this mean to you, an illiterate shepherd? What significance do you see in the flames—or do you know only that the divine has erupted into your ordinary reality? The very ground you stand on is holy; you take off your shoes and listen for the voice of Fire and Light.

Later, you will tell this strange small story to your children and grandchildren, never dreaming that countless generations will share your wonder. Centuries later, tongues of fire will lick at the heads of those gathered on the Day of Pentecost. This time the flame will hover over human flesh, but again the fire will neither consume nor even singe. The Living God is a fire that burns with fierce light...and yet he does not destroy that which he burns.

If we too are lit with a spark of God's fire, then we need not fear the loss of our identities. God says yes to you and me; his light allows us to see what is truly real, and his fire burns away only that which separates us from him. As the divine fire licks over us, our bodies and souls are united in a single, glowing flame. Like the stars, we too bear light.

Our heavenly Father wishes us to see, for he is the Father of light.
Accordingly, in the hidden depths of our spirit he eternally, ceaselessly,
and without intermediary utters a single fathomless word, and only that
word. In this word he gives utterance to himself and all things. This
word, which is none other than "See," is the generation and birth of the
Son, the eternal light, in whom all blessedness is seen and known.

—JAN VAN RUUSBROEC

You alone are a copy of the Being who is above all thought...a reflection
of the true Light. As you gaze at the light, you are transformed into it,
for its brightness shines in you.

—GREGORY OF NYSSA

42

6

Tree and Vine

The tree of life is the Lord Jesus Christ. The reason He is called a tree is to show how fruitful and beneficial He will be.

—JOHN BUNYAN

Spiritual vineyards...within whom all things are cultivated, all things are germinating, bearing fruit and bringing forth the spirit of salvation.

—BERNARD OF CLAIRVAUX

When I was young, one of my secret places was a sprawling old apple tree on the hill behind our house. I was neither agile nor daring when it came to tree-climbing, but with the help of an old gasoline can as a stepstool, I managed to boost myself high enough to scramble up into the branches. In the hollow where three great limbs joined together, I curled up with my cheek against the tree's rough skin. Breathing in the vinegary smell of the apples on the ground below, I would tip my head back so I could see the sky through the small oval leaves. The tree's branches demanded nothing of me; without question, without criticism, they simply held me.

For me, that tree was like a small, separate universe, another dimension from the demands of the real world. Safe within the tree's embrace, I had everything I needed; if I was hungry, I could stretch out my arm and grasp an apple; if I was bored, I found endless fascination creating tiny people out of twigs and the small, gnarled fruit; and if I was simply sad and lonely, I could wrap my arms around the tree's thick waist and be comforted. Like Shel Siverstein's Giving Tree, my apple tree gave to me freely of itself, fruit and wood, leaves and branches.

Ancient cultures knew what we may have forgotten: Trees have always been one of the best gifts given to humanity. Down through the centuries, trees have yielded great bounty: food and homes, tools and containers, medicines and vehicles, shelter in winter and shade in summer—not to mention simple beauty. The pre-Christian Celts worshiped trees as living beings endowed with the life-giving image of divinity. These long-ago people perceived trees as having supernatural power, spiritual strength that was an integral part of trees' physical reality.

For the Celts, each ash or willow or oak reflected the reality of the Tree of Life, an immense and living entity involved in both the creation of the universe and its ongoing structure. This divine tree connected the spirit world and the physical, for its roots were wrapped deep in the earth, while its branches were in the heavens.

The Hebrew Old Testament also speaks of a Tree of Life. It grows in Genesis's Garden of Eden, hinting that eternal life may yet be possible, despite our separation from God. The Book of Proverbs connects this mythic tree with God's eternal blessings: "…the fruit of righteousness is the tree of life" (11:30).

The New Testament uses the metaphor to describe Christ (Rev 2:7; 22:2). Christ's image reflects the Celts' mythic tree, "for by him all things were created…," says the apostle Paul in his letter to the Colossians, "and in him all things hold together" (1:16–17). Like the Celtic Tree of Life, Christ leaps between the spiritual and physical worlds. At the incarnation, the omnipotent and omnipresent Deity poured into the limitations of flesh and blood, "true God from true God," as the Nicene Creed affirms, and yet a specific man, Jesus of Nazareth. Through him, promises the New Testament, we too can experience the divine life that never ends.

In yet another letter, the apostle Paul speaks of the living, reciprocal relationship humans have with Christ, the Tree of Life: We do not simply pluck the fruit from the tree; instead, we become functioning parts of the tree's being. We bear its fruit. Jesus is the tree's root (Rom 15:12), says Paul, and we are "grafted" on so that we may "partake of the root and fatness of the olive tree" (Rom 11:17).

The Judeo-Christian tradition was not the only one to see glimpses of the divine in leaf and fruit, bark and branch. The Greeks' Dionysus, the god of wine, was also the god of trees, referred to by Plutarch as "Dionysus of the tree"; Plutarch speaks of him as "teeming" or "bursting with sap and blossoms." For the Greeks, trees' amazing fertility was a godlike power.

When Jesus claimed to be "the true vine," he may have had Dionysus in mind, for the Greeks believed that Dionysus, god of the trees, was also the personification of the vine. His story was not so different from Jesus' own, since Dionysus was violently killed, then buried, and finally raised up whole once more, just as Christ would be.

The cult of Dionysus was an extravagant one of ecstasy and intoxication. By contrast, Jesus' claim seems as matter of fact as the grapevine that spreads along its trellis beside our house, while its brown roots twist firmly in the earth. "I am the true vine," Jesus said; "…you are the branches. Those who remain in me, and I in them will produce much fruit. Remain in me, and I will remain in you" (John 15:1, 4, 5 NLT).

This metaphor is less intellectual. Light and darkness, water and stone remain outside of us, something to be considered from the distance of our minds. This metaphor, however, is inclusive: Christ is the vine, but so am I, so are you. Life flows into life. No one can say where you begin and I leave off; we cannot draw the boundary line that marks the point where Christ is other than you and me. Together, rooted in this world, we lift our leaves into the spirit realm. The life-giving sap flows through us all.

Like so many divine metaphors, however, the image must be broken to allow for paradox; otherwise, even the tallest, greenest branches are too meager to carry God's living presence. As the First Epistle of Peter says, Christ—the Tree of Life, the living organism who connects the tangible world and the heavenly one—also "bore our sins in his body on the tree" (2:24). At the crucifixion, the tree, a metaphor for life and eternal abundance, becomes the symbol for death and separation from God.

And yet trees carry the story of the resurrection in their sap and cells. Each spring, the cold dead wood shoots out green life, then buds and bears new fruit. Out of death new life is born.

In the woods today, I sat on the wet, muddy root of an old sycamore tree. It was twisted around the dead trunk of a still older tree, and it was so gnarled and tattered that it looked half-dead itself. But when I tipped my head back, I saw the same tree's sunlit vault of green-tipped branches, like interlaced arches against the sky.

When full summer comes, I know the sycamore's leaves will unfurl their broad green hands, growing so thickly I'll barely be able to glimpse the sky through them. The thought of that dense foliage makes me smile, for I remember creating papier-mâché sycamore leaves as a child in Sunday school, glopping them onto a cardboard tree's branches and then sticking the paper figure of a tiny Zacchaeus into the thick green mess. When the class was done, the teacher led us in a song we all knew:

Zacchaeus was a wee little man,
And a wee little man was he.
He climbed up into the sycamore tree,
For the Lord he wanted to see.

As a child, I identified with short Zacchaeus. I knew what it was like to have big people block my view, and I wondered if he needed to stand on something to boost himself up into the sycamore, just as I needed to step on the gasoline can before I could reach a toehold in my apple tree. Once he managed to scramble up into the broad branches, I could imagine how he must have felt, high above the world that rejected him. The sycamore's patched and papery bark beneath his hands would not have judged him; the thick leaves pro-

47

tected him. Just as the apple tree gave itself to me, Zacchaeus's sycamore lent him its branches. They lifted him up above the obstructions of earthly life, high enough that he could look into the face of God.

The *Mabinogian,* the collection of Welsh myths, tells of a tall tree that grows on a riverbank, half in flames from "the root to the top," while the other half is green and thick with leaves. Today in the woods, my old sycamore did not burn with fire and light; it was neither the *Mabinogian*'s magic tree nor Moses' burning bush. And yet it spoke to me of my life's dual nature, the simultaneity of life and death, physical reality and the spiritual realm. Rooted in the physical loss and decay of this world, we are still one with a greater life, a life that draws nourishment from earth's mud and decay, and reaches up toward heaven. Together we grow high and higher, until we too reach up and touch the sky.

As the apple tree among the trees of the wood, so is my beloved....
I sat down under his shadow with great delight,
and his fruit was sweet to my taste.
—SONG OF SOLOMON 2:3 NLT

Out of the stump...will grow a shoot—yes, a new Branch bearing fruit
from the old root. And the Spirit of the Lord will rest upon him.
—ISAIAH 11: 1–2 NLT

7

Food

You who are the angels' food...pasture the starving within your sweetness, for you are sweet without trace of bitterness.

—CATHERINE OF SIENA

Jesus took the bread, gave thanks and broke it, and gave it to his disciples, saying, "Take and eat; this is my body."

—MATTHEW 26:26

On a long-ago spring afternoon, Jesus of Nazareth and some of his close friends took a boat across the Sea of Galilee to the empty hills on the other side. They were hoping to find somewhere green and quiet, somewhere they could escape the crowds that had been following them for days.

As they climbed the hills, the wind off the sea was cool against their skin, but the sun warmed their heads. At the top of a hill, they flung themselves down on the ground and lay on their backs beneath the sky. They mumbled back and forth for a few minutes about their wives and the fishing and the spring weather, and then one by one they fell silent. The only sounds were the whisper of their own breathing and the sharp, faraway cry of a sea gull.

But then they heard another noise, like the low muttering of a thousand human voices. When they got to their feet and looked down the shoreline, they saw not a thousand people, but five thousand, fifteen thousand if they counted the children, all coming their way, like a slow dark wave. The crowd had discovered their hiding place.

Jesus may have sighed to himself. "How will we feed all these people?" was all he said, like a busy housewife musing on what she has in her cupboard to feed unexpected guests.

His friends probably rolled their eyes and shrugged; their master's words were clearly meant to be rhetorical. But for some reason, one of Jesus' followers took the question seriously. He waded into the tide of people, asking everyone the same question: "Do you have anything to eat with you?"

After a while he climbed back up the hill to Jesus and reported, "There's a boy here who has five rolls and two fishes."

His friends must have looked at him as though he were saying something foolish and annoying, as though he were a child repeating a trivial, pointless fact in the middle of an otherwise serious occasion.

But Jesus said, "Bring the boy to me."

If we had been there to see Jesus take the boy's food, bless it, and begin to break it into pieces, we might have thought he looked like a child who plays "tea party" by offering a pretend feast of cracker crumbs to her friends. The boy's tiny morsels of food should have been no practical use to a crowd of so many.

But miraculously, as Jesus' friends passed out the food, more and more bread and fish appeared. In the end, there was plenty for everyone. Jesus did not offer the people merely a snack, something to tide them over until they could make the long walk home to something better; no, instead, the members of every family there were fed until they were full. And food was left over.

The next day, everyone was gossiping about the way Jesus had fed the crowd. In a world where hunger was common and plenty was something few had ever experienced, Jesus' miracle was as welcome and astounding as if he had stood on a hill in our own time and handed out fifty-dollar bills.

But Jesus told them, "Seek the food that lasts forever, the food of eternal life."

By this time, people had seen Jesus do so many strange and impossible things that they wouldn't have been surprised if he had produced a magical, marvelous source of food. So someone asked him, "Are you going to feed us with manna from heaven, the way Moses did?" They were trying to find a way to make sense out of Jesus, a way they could fit his actions into the life they lived.

"The truth is," Jesus answered, "what Moses did really wasn't all that important. God gives you the real bread from heaven. And the bread that God gives comes down from heaven and gives life to the world."

At that, the crowd began shouting, "Give us this bread. That way we could feed our families. We would never be hungry again."

Jesus must have smiled and shook his head. "I am the bread of life. The bread I give you is myself, this tangible human body you see before you. If you open your hearts to me, you will never be empty again."

Each of the miracles recorded in the Gospels seems designed to tell us something about the nature of God and his kingdom, but the people present for this miraculous meal were distracted by their longing for never-ending physical food. Unlike the people of Jesus' day, most of us live in a world where food is plentiful, and yet we too find our understanding clouded by our perceptions of food itself. In our land of plenty, food continues to be fraught with emotional meaning.

Many of us, myself included, sometimes lose sight of the connection between food and physical nourishment. We do not always eat to give our bodies what they need; instead, we eat to feed our hearts, the starved, needy core of our beings. When my morning is bleak and I lack motivation to begin my daily work, I turn with relief to a cup of coffee and a doughnut; when my day seems barren, lacking joy and fulfillment, I am comforted by a bowl of fudge ice cream before I go to bed; and when my life is simply too much for me, when I am tense and miserable and frustrated, I soothe my pain with starchy "comfort foods" as though they could offer me as much hope and meaning as any miraculous bread from heaven. In moments like these, food is no metaphor for God. Instead, it is a god in its own right.

But like all false gods, ultimately it fails to deliver what we need most. No matter how much we eat, the food never reaches the emptiness inside us. We're left feeling frustrated—and guilty.

Our culture is obsessed with dieting. Eat less fat; eat more carbohydrates; eat more vegetables; eat no carbohydrates; eat more fiber: The messages are constant and confusing. Whether we are driven by health concerns or the desire for a particular kind of beauty, few of us are emotionally or intellectually immune to this constant onslaught on our diets. As a result, our feelings about food become even more complicated. In the midst of our ambivalence, how can we find God's face still hidden within this metaphor?

Yet of all the metaphors for God, this is the only one that has been made into a formal sacrament. At the Eucharist, we eat real food; the pale thin wafers of wheat will be first broken down into simpler sugars by the saliva in our mouths and then will pass into our stomachs and intestines, where they will be digested in the normal way. And we claim that these bites of ordinary food are actually Jesus. How can we understand this claim, though, when our perception of physical nourishment has become so twisted and obscured?

We have forgotten what food really is. Food ties us to the earth, for everything we eat is given to us by the natural world around us. We act as though human beings were a separate, isolated life form, but in reality, the act of eating weaves our lives into nature's web of prey and predator, a web where each organism has a part to play. I live because of the lives of a million blades of wheat, a thousand cows, ten thousand chickens, a hundred thousand rows of green growing plants. The cells of all these lives have become a part of mine.

So when Jesus claimed that his flesh was food, he forever knotted the spiritual world with the concrete world we see and touch—the same world that we eat and digest. God is not "out there" somewhere, floating like an ethereal dream. Instead, he is flesh and blood; he is the bread we eat and the wine we drink. He nourishes us and becomes a part of our very cells.

In the Gospels, however, Jesus speaks bluntly: Food alone can never meet our truest needs. "Why do you waste so much energy pursuing something that will one day spoil and leave you empty?" he asks the crowd. The question applies to us today as much as it did to those who heard his actual voice. Our need to eat is a fact of life, and food is one of our surest pleasures—but ultimately, no matter why we turn to food, even the sweetest, darkest chocolate; the most nutritious bread made from only whole organic grains; the frozen packaged diet meal with the lowest possible calories—none of these can offer us eternal nourishment for our inner being. When we seek the symbol itself instead of the divine reality that lies beyond the metaphor, the symbol becomes a lifeless idol.

But if we look past our own culture's ideas about food we may yet find that this metaphor can give us a true picture of the divine. My Italian mother-in-law sees food as the central, most significant joy of nearly any day. She does not look at a meal and count calories or grams of carbohydrates, nor does she turn to food as a drug to comfort her anxieties or lift her spirits. Instead, for her each loaf of crusty bread, each dark olive gleaming with oil, each pale gold strand of pasta soaked in fresh tomato sauce simply speaks of pleasure and love, of variety and flavor, of family and home. She may not connect all this consciously to God, but she is convinced that food is more than a biological necessity; she knows that mealtimes are meant to be slow, sweet moments of togetherness and grace. Her meals are sacraments, symbols of love spaced throughout each day.

All too often, though, the frantic pace of our lives destroys our sense of mealtime as an opportunity for relaxation and closeness. Like closet alcoholics, we snatch our food on the run, as though we were engaging in some surreptitious sin; in the midst of our stressful days, we gulp down high-fat, high-sugar fast food with frantic, guilty pleasure. But if we allow ourselves to experience meals as moments of bounty and nourishment, without guilt about calories and fat, we too may be surprised to find that even the simplest meal tastes of God.

The Eucharist—the church's formal picture of Christ as food—is also called communion. This small meal is not meant to be taken alone, as a moment of private spirituality. Instead, it is the symbol of our unity, our dependence on one another. Together we eat the bread of life, and we who are the body of Christ are nourished. When the divine comes to us as food, then the spirit world becomes one with our very flesh.

Each metaphor for God is like a mirror we hold up to catch a glimpse of the divine image. When Jesus says, "I am the bread of life," he hands us a looking glass as clear as any other. Our human hands may have fumbled and dropped the mirror until it lies in broken pieces around us. But when we pick up even the smallest fragment and hold it high enough to catch the light of God, we see an image as sweet as strawberries, as satisfying as homemade bread, as bountiful as a family dinner.

This image does not remain outside us, though, a reality external to our own being. Instead, it becomes one with our blood and muscles, skin and organs, nourishing the intimate workings of our hearts. And through this same image we are connected to the living, breathing universe around us.

Open your mouths, Jesus says in the Gospels. *Don't be afraid. Eat God.*

It is a balanced meal that Jesus serves us, a feast that, in turn, gives us balance to serve others.

—JO KADLECEK

Our food is to feast our eyes on God. Our meal is to commune with God. This is the banquet God offers us: real food. This banquet meal we are invited to attend forever.

—ROBERT FABING

8

Bird

*He shall cover thee with his feathers, and under
his wings shalt thou trust.*

—PSALM 91:4 KJV

*As an eagle stirreth up her nest, fluttereth over her young, spreadeth
abroad her wings, taketh them, beareth them on her wings,
So the Lord alone did lead him.*

—DEUTERONOMY 32:11, 12 KJV

Walking in the woods today, I see a crow high above me, black wings
against the blue sky like an arrow. He pushes through the air, a strong
swimmer breasting the currents, climbing higher and higher. With a
thrill of vicarious pleasure, my heart rises with him.

I suspect human beings have watched birds with wonder and
envy since before the dawn of history. We who are weighed down by
our flesh, tied to the earth, have always longed to escape. Human
beings may be more intelligent, stronger; we may have found ways to
fly within vehicles of metal and glass—but a bird's fragile frame of
feathers and hollow bones carries it higher than we can ever venture
in our own bodies.

And yet birds prove that flight is possible; flesh and blood can
rise up on wings and sing. As ordinary as sparrows fluttering in the
dusty street, as common as robins calling to each other on spring
mornings, birds remind us that in the midst of the everyday experiences of life, we can be startled by grace. Birds speak to us of God's
spirit present in the incarnated world around us. Birds give us hope.

Poets often connect the divine with birds, and the Bible uses the same metaphor. In fact, Scripture speaks of God as a *mother* bird with the spread wings of a protective hen or female eagle (Ps 17:9; Matt 23:27). At creation, the Spirit of God brooded over the earth's dark waters, like a sleepy chicken nestling an enormous egg beneath her warm breast. I remember as a child burrowing under my mother's apron when I was scared, her cotton skirt soft against my face. In the same way, the divine pinions protect us when we take shelter under God's hovering wings (Deut 32:11–12).

We see wings as maternal, sheltering, nurturing—and yet we also connect them with flight, with liberation, with a miraculous triumph over gravity. A winged creature is like the angels, somehow closer to eternity's boundless freedom. The metaphor unites loving protection with the mind-opening inspiration of flight.

But the two qualities seem contradictory; I associate protection with limitation. As an adolescent, the very thing I had craved as a child, my mother's shelter, I now wanted to escape. My adult self vacillates between resenting and relishing the physical security my husband gives me. So long as it is mutual and reciprocal, I feel free to enjoy it, but I resent any implication that I am weaker or needier than he is. I want my independence, my freedom.

Human protection so often implies ownership as well; it speaks of a hierarchy of power that ultimately diminishes the weak. But the divine wing both fosters and frees; God simultaneously shelters me and lifts me higher. The Spirit broods over the earth in Genesis 1, creating, shielding, mothering—and the same Spirit flies from heaven to land on Christ's shoulder at his entry into manhood, a symbol of mystery and power.

The swift whisper of descending wings at Christ's baptism also bears good news: God has flown from heaven to dwell on earth. With the breathtaking stoop of a hawk that drops like a stone out of the sky, Christ wings his way into our earthbound lives.

When Gerard Manley Hopkins, the nineteenth-century poet-priest, compared Christ to a kestrel in "The Windhover," he wrote of the paradoxical "buckle"—that which bends and breaks, that which fastens together—tying the sacrifice of Christ's earthly life with his airborne valor: "My heart in hiding / Stirred for a bird,—the achieve of, the mastery of the thing!"

We stand in awe of birds' mastery of flight—but their achievement surpasses human abilities in other ways as well. They possess a sense we lack, a powerful internal navigation device. This mysterious organic mechanism allows them to wing their way across immense distances as purposefully as well-aimed arrows.

I read recently that birds navigate by a combination of things: the sun, the wind, the earth's magnetic field, their sense of smell, and the stars. Somehow the messages from all these factors are combined into a single sense of purpose. The author suggested that the bird's perception of journeying may be as if it were watching a film: Its wings supply the energy to "run the movie," while mentally it remains constant, unmoving. As humans, we perceive much of reality linearly, but in the bird's mind, the destination is not the faraway end of a long line that must first be traversed. Instead, the bird's goal is already there, coiled up inside its head; all it has to do is flap its wings as it listens to the sun and the wind, the earth and the stars, and the film will unroll.

Despite birds' visible presence in our familiar linear world, apparently they inhabit another reality. We may know this other world exists, but we cannot glimpse it with our naked eyes. Christ too has his place in ordinary human history—and yet he soars above all our attempts to define his life in purely human terms. In the Gospels, his quiet sense of direction indicates to us his awareness of a purpose beyond human ken. He navigated by the light of some extraordinary perception we cannot imagine. Did he possess an inner sense that allowed him to hear the whisper of starlight and the hum of the earth?

On the phone today, my mother tells me she heard God speak to her this morning. Unlike Christ, she has never indicated that she possesses any hidden insight into reality's mystery, nor is she given to hearing voices or seeing visions. So I am curious to know what happened.

She was alone in the house, desperately missing my father who is in the hospital, and to escape the silence, she went out to sit on the porch. The flowers were drooping in the heat, she noticed, but she didn't care. Today her beloved petunias and larkspurs, delphinium and ageratum meant nothing to her.

Dully, hopelessly, she longed for God's comfort. As she shaped the thought into a vague prayer, a streak of scarlet feathers flew out of the woods and perched a foot away from her on the porch railing. For several minutes the tanager sang there beside her—and it spoke to my mother of loveliness brave enough to sing in the face of mortality and danger. It spoke to her with God's voice.

"It happened once before," she says, and then she tells me another story.

This time it was the winter after a death in our immediate family. My mother was in the kitchen, looking out the window, feeling the dreary burden of a grief that's grown old and heavy. The outdoor world was harsh and cold, as frozen as her heart.

And then a cardinal landed on the bank beyond the window, a splash of crimson wings against the ice. This time too my mother glimpsed the undying sweet color that flies from the heart of even the coldest and deadest winter.

My mother, of course, doesn't speak with the language I've just used. She only takes three or four sentences to tell her stories. But when I think of her tanager and cardinal, I too catch a glimpse of a winged vision, and faraway I hear eternity's song.

***

Like Noah, sometimes I look out and find my world submerged, drowned beneath work and worries, the trivial responsibilities that flood my life. And then I imagine I open a window, like the one Noah made in the side of his ark. I hear the soft beat of wings, and I watch as the white bird flies free across the ruin of my life. When it comes back to me, it flutters over me so close I feel the brush of warm feathers. In its beak, it bears a newly budded twig.

In the same way, the Spirit of God flies to us with the promise of renewal, while its wings offer both eternal refuge and the limitless challenge of love. Tenderly, certainly, the divine bird sings of hope.

To what shall I liken you, Lord?
To the dove that feeds its little ones....

—MARIAN, THE LITTLE ARAB

Every time I hear a robin sing, I am filled with thankfulness and praise.

—MARGERY KEMPE

9
Lamb

John saw Jesus coming toward him and said,
"Look, the Lamb of God...!"

—JOHN 1:29

What my parents called the hedge was a really a tall line of trees that edged the field beyond our house. I built myself a playhouse there, a shelter of fallen trees where I could create endless stories inside my head. I was always the heroine of these stories, always admired and valiant and strong. In reality, of course, I did not possess any of these qualities.

One day when I was playing in the hedge, a small, plaintive noise disturbed my make-believe. My heart leapt; I was longing for a cat of my own, and one of my fondest fantasies was that I'd find an abandoned kitten in the hedge and be allowed to keep it.

When I went to investigate, though, I found not a kitten but a lamb, huddled next to the barbed wire that fenced the pasture on the far side of the hedge. The lamb was not the quick-legged, soft-fleeced creature I had seen pictured in nursery rhyme books, but a stodgy little animal with round sides and dingy wool. When it saw me, it began to bleat; gingerly, I put my hand through the fence, nervous that the lamb might bite me. Instead, it shoved its hard head against my hand. The rough heat of its hide surprised me.

The lamb's cries were so urgent and lonely that I hated to leave it. I sat beside it for an hour or more, keeping it company. When I finally left it there, my heart twisted with guilt and pity. I resolved to spend time with the lamb every day, but its desperate neediness and misery made me uneasy. What could I do to take care of it?

But the next day, the lamb was gone. I tried to tell myself it had found its mother at last, but when I looked across the pasture, I could see no smaller shape among the adult animals. Later, I asked my mother what she thought. "Maybe there was something wrong with the lamb," was all she said, but her words had an ominous ring. I did not ask her what she meant; I did not want to know.

I was comforted by a small, framed print my Sunday school teacher had given me for Christmas. The picture showed a tender-faced Jesus clasping a lamb against his chest as he made his way through rocks and thorns. Jesus liked lambs, I knew.

My interest in lambs and shepherds may have been what induced my mother to teach me the Twenty-third Psalm. "The Lord is my shepherd," I recited obediently. "I shall not want. He maketh me lie down in green pastures." I hoped he had provided a soft green pasture somewhere for the lost, helpless creature that still haunted my thoughts.

The shepherd metaphor for God is a dominant one throughout both the Old and New Testaments. God, like a loving and vigilant shepherd, guides and protects his people. For the long-ago nation of Israel, the symbolism was potent and clear.

Just as Native Americans' lives once focused on the bison, the lives of those who dwelled in Bible lands centered on sheep. Sheep provided food and clothing, and the economy depended on the success of the herds. A sheep was the animal the Bible's people knew best. When they heard the word "lamb," it would have brought an immediate image to their minds, not the sentimental, stylized picture on which we've been raised but a warm and breathing three-dimensional shape. They knew the sound a lamb makes when it calls to its mother; they had felt its thick wool between their fingers; and they had breathed in the lamb's odor, a mixture of grass and manure and lanolin.

And not only did they know the animal; they also knew the tasks of a shepherd. When Christ claimed to be the Good Shepherd who lays down his life for his sheep, his listeners would have understood the depth and meaning of this sacrifice, for they knew sheep were not very clean, not very bright animals, prone to wandering into danger and yet precious nevertheless.

If ancient Native Americans from the central plains had written the New Testament, I wonder if they would have compared Christ to a bison. They certainly wouldn't have picked a lamb, since a sheep would have been outside their cultural experience. In order for a metaphor to work, in order for it to have power, it needs to speak in images we comprehend.

Except for those of us who are sheep farmers, most of us have little daily experience with lambs. In fact, except for our pets, many of us these days don't live closely to animals at all. Though we drink milk and eat eggs and hamburgers, we've forgotten our intimate connection with the dumb, patient beasts who give us our food. But though we are often separated from farms and nature, we still choose to share our homes with dogs and cats, guinea pigs and birds. Can these domestic animals speak to us of God, the Creator of the universe—or are they too small and tame to work as a metaphor for the divine?

⸙

A few years ago, my husband brought home a small white rabbit as an Easter gift for our children. Thumper lived in a hutch in our backyard. She visited us inside fairly often, but since she showed an unfortunate tendency to nibble on electric cords, her social calls were limited and closely supervised. Every evening, the children took a treat out to her—cabbage leaves or carrot tops—and stroked her soft wiggly nose. As pets go, she wasn't particularly exciting, but she was a good first pet. She was soft and gentle; she never nipped or scratched or hurt us in any way.

One Sunday after church, while my son and I were feeding Thumper apple parings, he asked me thoughtfully, "Why do they call Jesus the Bunny of God?"

I started to laugh, caught myself, and asked him what he meant. He frowned. "Oh, no, I mean Lamb of God. I get those Easter animals mixed up."

The conversation made me smile for a long time. But I had to admit the phrase Bunny of God sparked my imagination. Bunnies and lambs aren't so very different, after all. Both *are* Easter animals, connected in my mind with spring and new life and sweet, innocent fertility. Both are gentle, harmless animals; neither of them is very bright. And despite their innocence and helplessness, both are often slaughtered.

For the New Testament authors, that last quality was what spoke to them of Christ the loudest: just as Christ gave his life on the cross, lambs were killed as a ritual sacrifice. The connection between the two must have seemed both obvious and amazing.

But sacrificial ritual plays no part in my life today, and so that aspect of the metaphor has less meaning for me. And yet I too am amazed when I think of Christ as my long-ago miserable lost lamb— or as Thumper, a small, soft bunny, a stupid, helpless animal dependent on my care. The metaphor seems so unlikely I suspect some would find it sacrilegious.

Metaphors like light and stone and wind speak to me of God— but an animal, whether a rabbit or a lamb or some other domestic animal, brings God suddenly closer to me. Now he is no longer inanimate and abstract; he is intimate and breathing. He is in my arms. He needs me. As I think the metaphor through, it takes me by surprise.

A lamb is a particularly odd symbol for Christ since Jesus also identified himself with the shepherd. If Christ is the Shepherd, then I am the lamb, the small creature the shepherd feeds and protects. According to the stereotypes I often use to think of God, this seems to make more sense: He is big, I am little; he is strong, I am weak; he is knowing, I am ignorant.

But Christ in the Gospel of John turns the metaphor upside down and inside out. He insists that the Shepherd of our souls is also the Lamb, the one lacking power and intelligence, the one who is used for others' ends...the ultimate victim. What a strange metaphor for the King of Creation to claim as an expression of his own identity.

But the metaphors we use for God are like a flickering dance between reciprocal partners: He is light and darkness; parent and child; king and servant. If we choose to see Christ as the Lamb, do the steps of this dance require that we be the shepherds? What would that mean?

If we are shepherds, then we depend on no single place for our lives. We have no permanent homes; instead, we are rootless, wanderers, pilgrims. If we settle somewhere, thinking to find security, then we threaten not only our own lives but the life of the Lamb who is our charge. Stability and stillness seem to offer rest and safety, the chance to accumulate treasures of both the heart and hand, but as our focus shifts from *being* to *having*, our lives coagulate. Fixed on one grazing ground, the Lamb's presence in our hearts is no longer free to grow. Ultimately, the divine presence is starved—and so are we, for as shepherds, our livelihood depends on the animal we guard.

It boils down to this then: As we dance with God, if we see ourselves as shepherds, then our job is to care for the Lamb. We protect his presence in our lives. In concrete terms, we give the divine reality space by allowing time for prayer and meditation and wonder. These may not seem like practical activities, particularly when our lives are crammed with responsibilities. But if Christ is the Lamb of God, then our lives are meshed with his. We have no greater responsibility than to shepherd his life in our hearts.

The Lamb does not only live within our own hearts, though. He is also outside ourselves, present in all those who are vulnerable and needy, those who have been made victims of our society, those who are poor or sick or lonely. "If you love me," Jesus told Peter in the Gospel of John, "then feed my lambs."

❦

As a child playing in the hedge, I liked to pretend I was invincible. The lamb's misery drew me, but it also made me uneasy; I was afraid its demands would be too much for me. And I did not want to acknowledge that my own heart echoed its cries.

Today, an adult, I often react to the Lamb's presence in my life in a similar way. The demands of those in need are so great that I am afraid to look directly at them. I'm equally reluctant to look straight into my own heart, for fear I'll see my own desperate vulnerability. It's far easier to look away, to focus on other images of God that demand less of me. And yet Jesus insisted we find his presence in the small, the victimized, the helpless. He is the Lamb of God.

This Lamb is no pretty storybook animal, though, as mild and insipid as milk. Instead, this baby creature, this victim, sits on a throne (Rev 22:1), shines with radiant light (Rev 21:23), and heals the entire world (John 1:29).

To him who sits on the throne and to the Lamb
be praise and honor and glory and power,
for ever and ever!

—REVELATION 5:13

Human Metaphors

God created humankind in his image,
in the image of God did he create it,
male and female did he create them.

—GENESIS 1:27 SCHOCKEN BIBLE

Against the infinity of the cosmos and
the silent depths of nature,
the human face shines out as the icon of intimacy.
It is here, in this icon of human presence,
that divinity in creation comes nearest to itself.

—JOHN O'DONOHUE

Gardener and Farmer

So should we make a spiritual use of natural things; and so turn earth
(as it were) into heaven....If men will but accept [these thoughts], and
be content to have them engrafted to their own gardens (their hearts and
minds) by the Husbandman's watering of them by his Spirit, they will
grow and blossom, and bear much good fruit, here and forever....
Which improvement the Great Husbandman grant thee....

—RALPH AUSTEN

The kingdom of heaven is like a man who sowed
good seed in his field....
The one who sowed the good seed is the Son of Man.

—MATTHEW 13:24, 37

The Gospel of John tells us that on Easter morning, a woman named
Mary of Magdala stood in a garden outside an empty tomb. Mary was
confused and upset. She did not know yet that it was Easter; she
thought the one she loved was dead, his body stolen. When she turned
and found a man beside her, she assumed he was the gardener.

She wasn't expecting to see Jesus, not after she'd see him die on
a cross. And something about the man must have *looked* like a gardener. Maybe he was tending the trees and plants, or maybe he was
simply bending and touching them with his hands, as though their
growth and well-being mattered to him.

If Mary had not been so distraught, perhaps she would have
remembered that one of Christ's favorite spots had always been a

garden; she may even have been with the other disciples on the night before the crucifixion, when Jesus prayed in the Garden of Gethsemane. But Mary was overwhelmed with grief and frustration; she had forgotten that Jesus had always loved the natural world, that he had even referred to himself as a farmer who sowed the kingdom of heaven. And so, until she heard his voice speak her name, Mary failed to recognize Christ. She did not realize that the gardener she saw was actually the undying presence of the divine.

The natural world is full of metaphors for God's presence, but nature speaks without words. God also comes to us through other symbols, using the human form to impose language and shape on nature's boundless imagery. Just as the gardener brings order and pattern to the beauty of the natural world, God gardens our hearts, leading us further and deeper into the divine presence.

The word *garden,* I learn from my *Webster's,* comes from an Old English word that means "enclosure." The root word is similar to the same Old English words that give us *guard* and *gird* and *ward,* words that speak of defense and a careful watching presence. A garden, then, is a space that is protected and enclosed; life can grow there, because it is defended against injury and danger. The gardener is the one who conscientiously watches over this sheltered patch of earth, the one who cares for it and cultivates it. As the poet Isaac Watts wrote in the eighteenth century,

> We are a Garden wall'd around,
> Chosen and made peculiar Ground;
> A little Spot inclos'd by Grace
> Out of the World's wide Wilderness.

If God is the gardener, then our lives become the places that are sheltered and nurtured by the divine. Surrounded as we are by the destructive forces of a society that is often warped, sometimes unjust, we are nevertheless enclosed by grace.

The author of Psalm 104 wrote of the ways the divine presence seeds our world with life and bounty.

> Praise the LORD, O my soul.
> O LORD my God, you are very great…
> the earth is satisfied by the fruit of his work.
> He makes grass grow…and plants….
> The trees of the LORD are well watered,
> the cedars of Lebanon that he planted.
> …may the LORD rejoice in his works. (vss. 1, 13, 14, 16, 31)

Clearly, the ancient poet saw God as the world's gardener.

This metaphor was meaningful to Jesus as well. The Gospel of Matthew records three stories Jesus told where he referred to himself as a gardener or farmer (ch. 13). In these parables, the "Son of Man" (the divine presence in human form) scatters his seeds profligately across the world. These seeds do not grow unhindered; apparently, God's garden is as full of weeds as any other garden plot, and like all young seedlings, the divine life in our world suffers from hot sun and poor soil conditions. Still, however, when the gardener plants a mustard seed, "Though it is the smallest of all your seeds, yet when it grows, it is the largest of garden plants and becomes a tree, so that the birds of the air come and perch in its branches" (vs. 32). The life sowed by the Spirit is fertile and spreading—and even the smallest of beginnings yields rich bounty. That which was sheltered and guarded so it could grow now offers its own shelter. In the same way, our human lives are caught up into God's purpose.

Jesus lived in an agricultural community; stories related to farming would have made sense to his listeners. For these working people, a farmer was a more sturdy and practical image than a mere gardener. A gardener may cultivate beauty from the land—but a farmer grows food; he depends on the land for his very livelihood. Later in the Gospels, Jesus referred to the world's "harvest" (Matt 9:37; John 4:35); the divine sower does not merely create flower gardens. Instead, his seeds produce a practical and prosaic crop that will yield food for the hungry.

When I look at God not only as a gardener but a farmer as well, the metaphor is deepened and widened. The word *farm* comes from altogether different roots than *garden*. These new Old English and Latin sources mean both "to empty or cleanse" and "to make firm, hold safe." The implications of these ancient words seem to demand a greater austerity, and yet they also offer reassurance. If our hearts must be weeded and ploughed (a painful process surely), they will nevertheless find a new security and stability. Ultimately, of course, the divine farmer will make our soil soft and fecund, ready to yield life and fruit.

Personally, I'm not much of a gardener. Like any creative endeavor, gardening requires both passion and discipline—and the only discipline I pursue with consistent zeal has to do with words rather than plants. But gardens speak to me nevertheless.

The secret aching blue of larkspur...the fire of geranium...the purple and crimson scents of lilac and peony...the golden tang of marigold: All these fill my senses with harmony, while they whisper of an unseen Gardener behind their beauty. And vegetable gardens— neat rows of ferny carrots...green teepees of beans...the sprawling hairy stems of zucchini vines—all shout out songs of bounty. They sing of the rich, quiet miracle of soil and seeds and fruit.

Some days, though, I am afraid to believe in miracles. Faith seems a delusion, an extravagant plunge from the tangible world's bleak safety down into the bright irrational chaos of dreams and fantasy. Like any good Westerner, I trust only that which I can observe with my five senses. But neither my senses nor my intellect can grasp the secret hidden inside a seed.

And so I find myself imagining that the Gardener of this fertile, miraculous world is walking toward me. He walks with slow, sure steps, as though his bare feet enjoy the cool damp soil. His brown fingers brush each frond and blade he passes, and his touch holds both love and joy. Watching him, I know he is delighted by his garden.

I am ashamed to let him see my own rough patch. The soil here is empty of any growth; the irregular rectangle holds only sharp rocks and course clods. Nothing grows except clumps of weeds. Between their thick stems, the earth is barren, cold, and hard. For years I have kept this rank piece of earth, always resolving that one day I will find the time to bring order out of the chaos. In the meantime, tall walls hide it from the view of passersby. No one suspects what lies within those carefully maintained barriers.

But now the Gardener is entering my secret plot of weeds and rubble. "My sister, my bride," he says to me, "you are a garden locked up....Your plants are an orchard of pomegranates with choice fruits...with every kind of incense tree, and myrrh and aloes and all the finest spices....Awake, north wind, and come, south wind! Blow on my garden, that its fragrance may spread..." (Song of Sol 4:12–14, 16).

As he speaks, I realize that fine-stemmed life has crept like green fur over my bleak garden patch. The stems shoot toward the sky and flowers tumble from their leaves. Trees I never noticed are heavy with fruit, and the air is filled with the heady sweetness of roses and apples. Has the Gardener created all this new rich bounty from my life's chaos—or was it here all along, somehow disguised? Either way, I sense the divine seeds still germinating in my heart. I can only wait to see what new life will spring forth in the seasons that come.

"Let my beloved come into his garden and taste its choice fruits," I whisper, and I hear him answer, "I have come into my garden, my sister, my bride" (Song of Sol 4:16; 5:1).

Who would have thought my shriveled heart
Could have recovered greenness? It was gone
Quite underground; as flowers depart....

And now in age I bud again,

75

. . .

These are thy wonders, Lord, of love,
To make us see we are but flowers that glide;
Which when we once can find and prove,
Thou hast a garden for us to bide.

—GEORGE HERBERT

O Jesus, all my good and my bliss! Ah me!
Thy garden make my heart, which ready is for thee!

—DUTCH CAROL

2

Housewife

As the eyes of a maid look to the hand of her mistress,
so our eyes look to the LORD our God.

—PSALM 123:2

And as thy house is full, so I adore
Thy curious art in marshalling thy goods.

—GEORGE HERBERT

On the wall by my backdoor hangs a drawing of a bent woman with a broom in her hand. The picture has the austere lines and sepia tones of a medieval woodcutting, but on her feet the woman wears fuzzy slippers that leave her heels bare, and a flowered apron is tied around her waist. Her lips parted with delight, she holds up one square, work-hardened hand. She has just found a lost coin in the pile of dirt at her feet.

The picture was a Christmas gift from my friend Sister Lois. I loved it because she gave it to me and because of its simple artistic style, but I never understood the drawing's meaning. I knew of course that it illustrated Christ's parable of the woman and the lost coin. I've known the story for as long as I can remember, but I still couldn't quite connect with the picture. What did it really mean to me? I felt I was missing the point.

I must have walked by that picture on my way in or out the backdoor for about a year before I finally understood. I stopped one day, my car keys in my hand, and stared at the drawing, while my mind ran over the Gospel's story once again. Then I hung up my keys and went to get my Bible.

The story is in the fifteenth chapter of Luke, in the middle between Christ's parables of the lost sheep and the prodigal son. All three stories illustrate the joy and relief God feels when we turn back to him. I don't remember the time I didn't know that God was the Good Shepherd searching for the lost sheep, and my Sunday school teachers made quite clear that just as the father ran out to greet his prodigal son, God welcomes us when we come back to him. God is a shepherd, God is a father; I was familiar with these metaphors. But no Sunday school teacher ever spelled out the parallel metaphor that is clearly there in Christ's story: God is a housewife.

I have never been a shepherd with a lost sheep, nor have I been the father of a wastrel son. But I am a housewife who loses things all too often, and I have swept my floor for a missing earring or searched the corners of my house for a child's toy. I identify with this metaphor. I can't walk by the picture now without sensing the warm reminder that I am loved. On the days when I feel lost and confused, I rely on the image of the divine housewife down on her knees, patiently searching the dusty corners until she finds me.

As a modern woman, however, I am often ambivalent about my role as a housewife. My husband and I struggle to divvy up the household chores fairly—but in Bible times, the division of labor was both clearer and less loaded with value judgments than it is today. Although the culture was undeniably patriarchal, taking care of a home was not considered insignificant and menial work. Wealthy households were enormous, and the woman who organized the physical needs of all these people had to use as much skill and intelligence as any modern-day corporate executive. She was the sort of woman described in Proverbs 31:

> She selects wool and flax
> and works with eager hands.
> She is like the merchant ships,

bringing her food from afar.
She gets up while it is still dark;
she provides food for her family
and portions for her servant girls.
She considers a field and buys it;
out of her earnings she plants a vineyard.
She sets about her work vigorously;
her arms are strong for her tasks.
She sees that her trading is profitable,
and her lamp does not go out at night.
In her hand she holds the distaff
and grasps the spindle with her fingers.
She opens her arms to the poor
and extends her hands to the needy.
When it snows, she has no fear for her household;
for all of them are clothed in scarlet.
She makes coverings for her bed;
she is clothed in fine linen and purple.
…She is clothed with strength and dignity.…
She speaks with wisdom,
and faithful instruction is on her tongue.
She watches over the affairs of her household
and does not eat the bread of idleness. (vss. 13–27)

The woman depicted in these verses is articulate and competent; although some of her tasks may be different from mine (I haven't grasped a spindle recently, nor have I planted too many vineyards), she juggles every bit as many responsibilities as I do. In fact, I'm a little intimidated by the strength and dignity that clothe her. I'm not sure I can measure up to her high standard.

But the point here, I think, is not to shame women by holding up an impossible paragon of virtue for them to emulate. Instead, the writer is taking "women's work" seriously; the author is honoring the strength and intelligence needed to run a household.

Our culture has taught us to see housework as menial and demeaning, but when I look up "menial" in my *Webster's*, I find that the original word had nothing to do with inferiority; instead, it comes from Latin roots meaning "to remain, to dwell." This sense of stability and permanence surely means that our household chores reflect aspects of the divine nature, "with whom is no variableness, neither shadow of turning" (Jas 1:17 KJV).

Psalm 123:2 puts God in the housewife's role, the mistress of her household, while we are one of her servants, watching her as we wait for her mercy. Here God is the one who manages a complicated household; like the woman in Proverbs 31, God provides nourishment for us, clothes us, and opens loving arms to us. God watches over our affairs and is intimately involved in the physical details of our lives.

The seventeenth-century poet George Herbert used this image in his poetry when he wrote that God's "cupboard serves the world: the meat is set, where all may reach." God, like any good housewife, keeps her family fed. God attends to our daily needs. He spreads our tables with bounty that is always available.

When my daughter was younger, she asked me to read again and again a picture book called *Old Dame Counterpane*. The book tells the story of a comfortable, elderly housewife who stitches up the world every day. It begins with these words:

> Old Dame Counterpane
> In her work clothes,
> The longer she rocks,
> The longer she sews,
> The longer she sews,
> The greater earth grows,
> Old Dame Counterpane
> In her work clothes.

As the book continues, Old Dame Counterpane works through the day and night, sewing all of life's lovely details, including "you and me"—and then, "The night being over, She starts again."

"She's God," my daughter pointed out to me. "Old Dame Counterpane is God." Unlike her mother, who had walked blindly past a portrait of the divine for nearly a year, my daughter's young eyes were clear of gender stereotypes.

And as a child, she understood the blessing of repetition as well. I am often discouraged when, like Dame Counterpane's, my work asks me to start all over again. But children delight in life's repeating patterns. Perhaps they draw comfort from the small repetitions of life—like making breakfast and helping Mommy do the laundry—because they understand, unconsciously of course, that in a similar way God is creating their universe, again and again and again, world without end.

God ceaselessly attends to the repetitive details of our lives; he is present in the enduring cycles of exhalation and inhalation, day and night, birth and death. "Repetition," wrote Søren Kierkegaard, "is the daily bread which satisfies with benediction." The Japanese poet Santoka expressed this same sense of the divine in actions that repeat themselves: "In the never-ending sound of water you will always find the Buddha."

As grownups, however, most of us have forgotten the value of repetition. I suspect that fact has something to do with the way we see time. In our minds, time is a linear thing, and we approach our work with that same beginning-middle-end framework. We are goal oriented; when we attack a specific task, we tend to have the final outcome firmly in our imaginations. If that outcome then becomes undone, as happens over and over with housework, we feel as though we are losing ground. Naturally, we're frustrated.

But linear time, physicists tell us, may not be as absolute as we have always assumed. In fact, some theoreticians now believe that time does not exist at all anywhere outside the biological brain. Whatever time's true nature, theologians and mystics have always affirmed that another reality lies beyond time's boundaries. Their word for this reality is eternity.

Before the invention of timekeeping devices, earlier civilizations perceived time as being cyclical rather than linear as we do today.

Since cycles can repeat endlessly, perhaps this view of time actually came closer to a concept of eternity. At any rate, housework's never-ending routines fit more comfortably into this scheme. Just as the earth sinks into decay each winter only to be born again each spring, our households go through ceaseless circles of chaos and renewed order.

Divine grace lies in our lives' everyday cycles. Like Old Dame Counterpane, God daily expresses his creativity anew, over and over and over. "Because of the LORD's great love," wrote the author of the Book of Lamentations, "we are not consumed, for his compassions never fail. They are new every morning" (3:22–23). Like any good housewife, God endlessly, routinely, lovingly works through the daily details of our lives.

Many women do noble things,
but you surpass them all.
—PROVERBS 31:29 KJV

Even life's tiny everyday occurrences...the puddle of milk on the floor,
the worn surface of the cutting board—offer you a chance
to contemplate and learn....
—GARY THORP

3

The Poor

We need the eyes of deep faith to see Christ in the broken body and dirty clothes under which the most beautiful one among the sons of men hides.

—MOTHER TERESA

The Lord made himself poor for us in this world. This was the culminating point of poverty.

—FRANCIS OF ASSISI

Long ago in the thirteenth century, a young man named Francis was working hard in his father's business when a poor man came through the door. "Please help me," the beggar whispered, "for the love of God."

Francis's father was a busy merchant with no time or compassion for those in need. "Get rid of him," the father told his son, and Francis obliged.

But afterward, the beggar's face haunted Francis. Something in the man's eyes would not leave Francis in peace. It insisted on his attention, his love even. Finally, Francis could no longer resist. Ignoring his father's disapproval, he began to search the streets of his city, looking for the beggar. That undefined something he sensed in the man's poverty was still tugging at Francis's heart. When he found the beggar at last, he poured a stream of silver coins into the man's thin, grimy hands.

Technically, of course, the coins belonged to Francis's father, but that didn't stop Francis from giving away all the gold and silver he could. From that day on, he gave everything he had to anyone who asked. His father was enraged by his son's actions and vowed to disown him, but Francis only shrugged. "My true father is God," he told his father, "who lives in heaven. He gives me all I need, so I'll give back to you not only all your money, but all my clothes as well."

Francis stripped the fancy clothes off his body and walked away naked. "I'm free," he said over his shoulder. He spent the rest of his life serving those in need, sharing their poverty. He found in them the image of Christ—that same irresistible *something* that had called to him from the face of the beggar.

<hr>

The story of Francis of Assisi is both beautiful and outrageous. His actions were so extreme, so childlike in their simplicity and audacity, that we often assume he offers the twenty-first century no realistic call to action.

And yet Francis understood that possessions tend to possess us. All the things we own…houses and cars, blue jeans and sweatshirts and socks and underwear and dress clothes and shoes, books and CDs and stereos, computers and telephones and washers and dryers and refrigerators and toasters, knickknacks and pictures and houseplants and furniture…ultimately, all these adhere to our souls. We are often so preoccupied with the maintenance of all these *things,* our spiritual nerve endings so encrusted and numb, that we can no longer touch the divine skin.

But those who are poor in our world, those whose lives have been pared down to the bony essentials, call us to strip ourselves free so we can once again touch God. The poor have been robbed of all earthly comforts (the many subterfuges like home and status and belongings the rest of us use to make ourselves feel secure); they have no choice but to walk naked and real into God's presence. Their insistent voices hold the same *something* that called to Saint Francis from the beggar he had rejected.

"Blessed are you who are poor," Jesus said (Luke 6:20), "for yours is the kingdom of heaven." But then he goes still further;

"Whenever you did for one of the least of these...you did for me" (Matt 25:40). Not only are the poor blessed, but they are Jesus himself, the divine with skin on.

Jesus, God in human form, lived his own life on earth without wealth or belongings, and the crucifixion was his ultimate identification with those who are desperately needy. On the cross, Christ was stripped of everything—his clothes, his dignity, even his knowledge of God's presence.

We are attracted to most symbols for God. Metaphors from nature may be intimidating at times, but they are still beautiful; in most human metaphors for God we catch a glimpse of something loveable and sympathetic, some human quality we recognize and appreciate. But the poor make us uneasy. People who lack food, proper hygiene, and education are seldom pretty; how can we see God's image in such ugliness and despair?

Perhaps the poor make us so uncomfortable because their very existence challenges the way we live. Inside our well-furnished houses, beneath our warm, comfortable clothes, we are no different from those who are poor and desperate. We are all human; we are all needy and vulnerable. But that fact may frighten us, and so we turn away from the presence of the poor. If we ignore those who are oppressed and in pain, we won't have to face our own hidden poverty.

And yet, according to the Gospel of Matthew (5:3), even the poor in spirit are blessed. Mother Teresa, who spent her life serving India's needy, spoke of the desperate spiritual poverty she saw in the Western world—and the face of Jesus looked out at her from beneath the guise of wealth and plenty. She wrote: "We need to be poor in heart to see Jesus in the person of the spiritually poorest. Therefore the more disfigured the image of God is in that person, the greater will be our faith and devotion in seeking Jesus' face and lovingly ministering to him."

Somehow God's presence is to be found even where He seems most absent.

As a young woman, I spent about eight months in Tijuana, Mexico, working in an orphanage there. Mexico is a poor country; Tijuana is an ugly, desperate city; and the orphanage was a place of dust and broken windows. The toilets seldom flushed; the plumbing often failed altogether. American churches donated huge bags of rice, flour, and beans to feed the children; I helped pick the pebbles out of the rice and beans, and strained the tiny insects out of the flour. When I went to bed, I'd lie and watch the dark flicker of rats running along a ledge beneath the ceiling; I scratched my fleabites and listened to the rustle and bump of the rats dropping through a hole into the pantry.

And yet I remember my time at the orphanage as one of the happiest of my life. Living with the children there, I felt a sense of belonging and purpose I had never experienced. I barely noticed the warm, unwashed odor of their bodies; I only saw the flash of their white smiles against brown skin. I was exhausted every night when I went to bed, but the Holy Spirit's presence seemed nearly tangible in the air around me.

Back in the United States, I sought to repeat the experience by becoming a social worker in an inner-city crisis center. I worked with people who were homeless, who were mentally ill, who were angry and frustrated by their poverty. Although I enjoyed these people—and yes, I did see Christ in their naked honesty—I did not find that same sense of belonging I had experienced in Tijuana. My clients needed help— and yet they resented those who offered it. Some days I was hurt and angered by their rejection. I could not see how different my role as a social worker was from what I had done in Mexico. In the crisis center, I did not eat and sleep with the people I served. Instead, I wore professional clothes and sat behind a desk in an office; while I went out for lunch with my coworkers to our favorite café, my clients waited for me in a hot narrow room crowded with metal folding chairs. Their anger and resentful shame should have come as no surprise.

I could not see my own hypocrisy and self-righteousness, though. I thought I wanted to serve the poor. In fact, I wanted to use them. I wanted to nourish my own empty heart with the food of their gratitude; I wanted to enjoy their honesty and savor their vulnerability, while keeping myself separate and safe in my own world.

When we catch a glimpse of God in those who are poor, we are not meant to sit back and simply admire it. Other divine metaphors may speak to us through their essential beauty; we can meditate on these symbols' attributes and learn more about the nature of God— but there is nothing divine at all about human suffering and need. The poor are not blessed because they possess some wonderful spiritual quality; instead, they are blessed because God hears their cry. God has identified himself with them through Christ, so that he can call to us through their voices. They are a challenge to our smug self-sufficiency, a voice that demands our response. God does not ask us to institutionalize and appreciate human misery from a safe distance. He calls us to do all we can to put an end to it.

Jesus took on poverty not because it is *good* to be poor—but because of his mission on earth. Native American theologian Achiel Peelman writes: "He is not a God who loves suffering, but a God who commits himself faithfully with respect to the total well-being of the world he has created."

The good news Jesus brought to earth is not a private transaction between God and me. Instead, I have to give myself away for the kingdom of Heaven, just as Christ did. This is the divine voice that calls to me from the poor. It's the same message that John the Baptist shouted: "Prepare a pathway for the Lord's coming! Make a straight road for him!...If you have two coats, give one to the poor. If you have food, share it with those who are hungry....Don't extort money and don't accuse people of things you know they didn't do. And be content with your pay...." The implication is that when we practice social justice, "then all people will see the salvation sent from God" (Luke 3:4, 11, 13, 14, 6 NLT). John knew that Jesus had not only brought a spiritual message to earth; Jesus had also brought real and practical salvation to the needy and oppressed. Jesus would change the world forever by showing us how to love one another.

Touching God through divine symbols may seem like a mystical, otherworldly practice—but in fact, we can only grasp this particular symbol in concrete, tangible ways. This metaphor lays claim to our checkbooks and closets, our pantries and our time. It asks that we learn all over again the childhood lesson of sharing. It demands that we truly see the needs of those around us.

⸙

Last night I visited a nearby nursing home where a friend of mine helps care for her mother. While we sat in the lounge and talked, a woman in a wheelchair came creeping toward us, her feet fluttering across the floor like little paddles. She was dressed only in a hospital gown, and her face was empty and vacant.

"Hello, Dorothy," my friend said. "Want to join us?"

Dorothy pushed herself up close to our chairs and looked into our faces. "Sure," she said after a moment, her voice so soft and gentle I could barely hear it. Her face had the innocent emptiness of a very young baby's.

She was stripped of everything—home, possessions, clothing, family, memory. Her poverty was so deep and intense that my heart ached. I thought I had nothing I could share with her to comfort her.

My friend stroked the gray hair away from Dorothy's worn face. "You're so beautiful, Dorothy," she said.

For just a moment, Dorothy's entire being seemed to change, like a baby's does when a smile suddenly lights its face. "Sure," she whispered. Pure, undiluted delight radiated from her, the same joy that must have shone from the face of Francis of Assisi when he ran naked from his old life.

From those who are as utterly poor as Dorothy I learn what Abraham Joshua Heschel wrote: "Just to be is blessing. Just to live is holy." And when I reached out for Dorothy's yellow, wrinkled hand, I knew I was touching God.

The Poor

I was hungry and you gave me something to eat, I was thirsty and you gave me something to drink, I was a stranger and you invited me in, I needed clothes and you clothed me, I was sick and you looked after me, I was in prison and you came to visit me....I tell you the truth, whatever you did for one of the least of these...you did for me.

—MATTHEW 25:35–36, 40

Pray lovingly like children, with an earnest desire to love much and to make loved the one that is not loved....When we handle the sick and the needy we touch the suffering body of Christ.

—MOTHER TERESA

4
Host

A man prepared a great feast and sent out many invitations.
When all was ready, he sent his servant around
to notify the guests that it was time for them to come....
After the servant had done this, he reported,
"There is still room for more."
So his master said, "Go out into the country and lanes
and behind the hedges and urge anyone you find to come,
so that the house will be full."
—LUKE 14:16–17, 22-23 NLT

At the end of my yoga session last week, our leader asked us to lie on the floor while she directed us through a guided imagery. The exercise was designed to help us relax, emotionally, physically, mentally. The words she used went something like this:

Imagine you are walking along a winding country lane. Your journey has been long and strenuous, and now your mind and muscles are weary. At some points along your path you have been afraid, lonely, overwhelmed. But now you are filled with anticipation. You know that just ahead is a place where you can rest. The host of this rest-house has prepared a place just for you, a safe place, a place where you can be refreshed body, mind, and soul.

As your reach the crest of a small rise in the lane, you see the guest-house in the valley below. It is a large, rambling house, filled with windows, a broad porch running around it on all sides. Your steps quicken as you hurry down the hill.

Your host stands at the door, eager to welcome you. Her arms are spread wide; as you climb the porch steps, she pulls you into her sheltering embrace. With a sigh, you lean your head on her soft breast.

"Your friends are on their way," she tells you. "They'll be joining you here later. I have plenty of room for everyone, and I've been baking all day. Later, we'll feast together—but for now, come in...rest...I have your room all ready for you."

She leads you up the staircase to the second floor, where she opens a door. When she steps aside to let you enter, you see tall windows that look out over green hills; a four-poster bed is piled with handmade quilts and pillows. Everywhere you look are signs of your host's loving preparation: Fresh flowers bloom on the bedside table; a fire crackles in the fireplace; your favorite fruits and pastries spill from a wicker basket; and the book you've been wanting to read for weeks waits for you on your pillow.

"Rest now," your host says. "Take all the time you need. I'll be close by if you should need anything."

With another deep sigh, you sink down on the thick rug in front of the fireplace. Your host tucks a quilt around your shoulders and then tiptoes away. Curled up like a child, you know you are completely safe. Your host has created a place where you can rest. You are no longer alone; you no longer need to strive. Here you will have everything you need to enjoy yourself and be restored.

As you watch the flicker of the fire, your gaze follows the sparks as they float upward. Your eyelids grow so heavy, though, that they fall shut. Secure, warm, relaxed, you allow yourself to drift into sleep, knowing that many pleasures await you when you wake.

My reaction to this relaxation exercise was not quite what the leader had intended. By the time her voice faded away, tears were running out of the corners of my eyes into my ears. I wanted that guesthouse to be real; I yearned for the host to welcome *me*. When I examined my reaction, I realized how solitary I've felt lately, how hard I've been struggling to deal with my life's issues, how tired and restless and lonely I've been.

I suspect those feelings are a part of the human condition. Our world today is full of the dispossessed—refugees and homeless people who lack an actual, physical shelter. The rest of us may live in comfortable homes, physically secure, and yet as close as we may be to our friends and family, ultimately we are all alone. At some level, deep in our hearts, we know we are detached from the rest of humanity. We long for a host, someone who will welcome us and take us in.

⁂

Dante Alighieri, the thirteenth-century poet, knew what it meant to be an outcast. Because he had sided with the losing faction in the fierce political war that raged in his home city of Florence, he found himself condemned to exile. He could never go home again.

For the next twenty years, he wandered around Italy. Tolerant noblemen offered him sanctuary from time to time, and Dante found many temporary residences; eventually, he always grew restless and moved on. He was disillusioned with politics; he wanted freedom from factions; he longed for peace. But not many thirteenth-century Italians saw things the way he did. Even as still another generous host opened his home to the exile, Dante felt uncomfortable and uneasy. He longed for home—and yet his old home no longer existed. He had nowhere to call his own.

For years, his life was lonely and restless. The only real sanctuary he had was his own mind, where he struggled to compose his great epic, the *Divine Comedy*. But no one, not even a creative genius like Dante, can live completely in an intellectual world. Our hearts and bodies yearn to be at rest as well.

At last, however, Dante found a host who offered him more than a temporary residence; this man, Guido Novella, opened his own home and made a place for Dante that was all his own. At the court in Ravenna, Dante found his own space, a place of privacy and comfort. Within this sanctuary, Dante was free to grow. His literary creativity, that most essential part of who he was, was appreciated and nurtured. He was not merely tolerated, with the grudging sense that the time

95

would come for him to move on; instead, he was pulled into Ravenna's life, welcomed, granted both shelter and dignity. Here, Dante found not only a guesthouse; he found a home. Finally, he could complete the last part of the *Divine Comedy—Paradiso,* his vision of our eternal home, the soul's bright refuge.

⚜

Like Dante, my soul longs for someone to give me a haven. If I apply the metaphor to the divine presence in my life, then God becomes my Host, the one who flings open his doors to me in welcome. When I feel desolate and alone, he offers me his generous presence as my home. As Guido Novella did for Dante, God gives me a place in his kingdom that is all my own, a place where I can claim the dignity of my truest identity.

Perhaps the divine Host comes to me with such openhearted graciousness, because he grasps my plight so well—for he is both the divine Host *and* the divine Guest. The etymology of the word *guest,* oddly enough, tells me that both *guest* and *host* come from the same Latin root: *ostia,* a word that means "stranger, an alien." From a linguistic perspective then, *host* and *guest* are two halves of a reciprocal dyad. *Both* words mean "stranger."

Like so many metaphors for the divine, this one can also turn itself inside out: *host* and *guest* are two halves of a whole, and we who are God's guests are also his host. In the seventeenth century, author Anthony Horneck wrote, "How often…hath thy great Master attempted to enter into thy heart and to make that his guest-chamber," and Teresa of Avila speaks of serving our "holy Guest." Both images spring from Christ's words as recorded in the vision of Revelation: "Look! Here I stand at the door and knock. If you hear me calling and open the door, I will come in, and we will share a meal…(3:20 NLT).

When I was a child, a picture hung in my parents' living room that showed Christ knocking on the heart's door. The world outside that door was painted in somber shades of sepia and umber; even the vegetation that sprang up around Jesus' figure looked threatening and dark. As I looked at that painting, I would feel a shiver of horror, for I imagined myself standing all alone, shivering and scared in front of that tight door. I could relate to those feelings of loneliness and terror, but I could not imagine a God who was so vulnerable.

But if my life is shut tight, if I find myself revolving ceaselessly around my own selfish concerns, then I am on the inside of that forbidding door. My heart is closed to anything that lies outside my own interests. I have rejected those around me, including the divine Guest, the Host who is present in all outcasts.

Deep in our hearts we too may sometimes feel rejected and excluded, but the divine presence has joined himself to our condition. We are aliens and outcasts—and as our Host, he has identified himself with us. In the Gospel of Matthew, Jesus says, "Foxes have dens to live in, and birds have nests, but I, the Son of Man, have no home of my own, not even a place to lay my head" (8:20 NLT). Through Christ, God comes to us as someone who is homeless. He understands the forlornness of our human condition. We are no longer alone.

The First Epistle of Peter refers to Christ as an outcast, "rejected by the people" (2:4 NLT). This book of the New Testament speaks to those who are also outsiders; the epistle's first verse is addressed to people who are "exiles," "scattered" (Amplified Bible). They are temporary residents, visiting aliens in strange lands.

The words used by the epistle's author are the same ones historically used for the Diaspora, Jews who were spread across the earth, cut off from their homeland. Here, however, Peter connects us all to the Jews' plight: At a spiritual level, we are a transitory people, pilgrims passing through this world. We are sojourners yearning for home.

If reality extends beyond the world we see and touch, then perhaps some part of us senses those wider horizons beyond our perception. We long for something more, something fuller and more complete, something beyond our ability to grasp. This yearning is like a spiritual itch we can never quite reach. "Our hearts are restless, Lord, until they find their rest in you," wrote Saint Augustine. We long for home—and the divine Host holds out his arms and welcomes us to a "spiritual house" (1 Pet 2:5).

What's more, the New Testament epistle indicates we are not merely passive recipients of this welcome. Instead, we are swept up into it. We the guests now become the "living stones" that build this home for the spirit.

⸻

I too, like Dante, have been hosted in such a way that I was both sheltered and freed, nurtured and respected. For instance, when I visit my mother-in-law's home, I find there a place of rest and comfort. I relax in the knowledge that in her house I have room to be myself—and for once I don't have to make decisions or juggle jobs. I am free to come and go, to work or rest, knowing that either way I am loved and welcome.

For my mother-in-law, creating domestic order and bounty comes as naturally as breathing. She's no martyred drudge, though; instead, she opens her home to others with assurance and pride. When I'm a guest in her home, even my dirty laundry magically reappears in my suitcase, clean and neatly folded. She offers me a second home, a home where I am surrounded by gracious liberality. Back in my own house, as I put away my clothes, I find they have absorbed the odors of sauce and garlic and vegetable soup. To me, they smell like the word *welcome*.

But *host* has another meaning as well: It is the bread of Eucharist, the divine sacrifice. This word also derives from *ostia*, that same Latin root that gives us *host*'s other meanings. Perhaps the best hosts, the ones like my mother-in-law who make us feel truly at home, always give a part of themselves away.

To identify with us as outcasts and wanderers, Christ our Host not only opened his arms in welcome. He went still further and sacrificed himself so that we would no longer be refugees and strangers. Our divine Host gave himself completely. And as his guests, we each find that sheltered space where our hearts can grow.

Host

In my Father's house are many rooms; if it were not so, I would have told you. I am going there to prepare a place for you. And if I go and prepare a place for you, I will come back and take you to be with me....

—JOHN 14:2–3

The Chinese philosopher Meng-che said: "When you hear someone talk, look into his eyes—what can remain hidden there?" A man may say "Welcome," but in his eyes we can read: "Don't stay too long, I'm busy," ...but when Jesus says "Welcome," his eyes make you believe you will be safe with him.

—AUSPICIUS VAN CORSTANJE

5
Child

Today in the town of David a Savior has been born to you;
he is Christ the Lord.
This will be a sign to you: You will find a baby....

—LUKE 2:11–12

And the child grew and became strong;
he was filled with wisdom, and the grace of God was upon him.

—LUKE 2:40

When it comes to interacting with young children, I know two categories of people—those who tolerate babies and those who adore them.

The first kind is generally fond of the specific babies to whom they are related, but they feel no overwhelming attraction to young children in general. If they have raised their own babies, as many of my friends have, when they look back on the days when their lives centered on young children, they feel a wholehearted and unabashed relief that those years are over. They much prefer to be the parents of older children. Unlike babies, older offspring leave you room to think...to pursue your own life...to go to the bathroom in luxurious privacy.

The second category of people, however, appear oblivious to the infant's demanding and irrational nature. These are the people whose eyes light up whenever they spot a small, round face peeping out of a stroller. They're the ones who begin to coo whenever a young child comes within ten feet; they reach out their arms to strangers' babies, yearning to hold small bodies against their breasts; and if they can no longer hope for babies of their own, then they count the years until they become grandparents.

As the mother of school-age children, I treasure the long, quiet weekdays when I am free to write and read, to grow professionally, intellectually, and spiritually in ways I never could when I had preschoolers. And yet, I have to confess—I belong to the second category of people: I love babies. At church I cannot tear my eyes away from the small child who peeks over her father's shoulder from the pew in front of me. When my fascination becomes too apparent, I feel an elbow dig into my side. "Mom!" my thirteen-year-old hisses, and I meekly turn my eyes away from the tiny, starfish hands, the sweet curve of a baby cheek, the friendly wonder in eyes that are still learning to recognize the world's shapes and meaning.

If I had followed the inclinations of my heart, I'd probably be one of those pale, worn women I see occasionally with a troop of children trailing ahead and behind, ranging in age from a three to thirteen, while she lugs another solid little body on her hip. For medical reasons, though, I had to stop after I had my three children.

I'm rational enough to know that three is a perfectly fine number of children. I can't consider myself cheated or suffering from some great and unmerited loss, and I'm even able to recognize that truthfully, I'm far happier with my life now than I was as the mother of babies and toddlers. And yet I'm still filled with yearning whenever I see a young child. At night I dream of finding babies on my doorstep or discovering that I'm about to have one more child after all. When I wake up, I feel as though I've lost something important, as though inside my heart a secret, restless emptiness can never be filled.

I've begun to tolerate this longing the way you learn to live with some painful but minor chronic illness. Only recently have I begun to suspect that these feelings have spiritual significance. Maybe the child for whom I long is really another metaphor for the divine—the Christ Child.

Child

I find many times that the most powerful divine symbols are the ones present in my life without me even realizing. It's as though God has infiltrated my life without me noticing; he slipped in when I wasn't looking—and then suddenly, like windows opening to the light, these ordinary aspects of my life are flung open, driving the shadows away to reveal a glimpse of something greater and deeper, something that was there all along. My longing for a baby was this sort of experience; one day the familiar, nearly tedious ache sprang apart to show me God's face. And I'd guess something similar happened in my youngest daughter's mind when she was very young.

As a three-year-old, my daughter loved anything that was a baby. The sight of a kitten or a puppy or a human baby filled her with over-flowing delight. She was even excited about the tiny mini-bagels our church served after the Sunday service. They too were "babies," too little and precious for her to eat. Instead, she would rock them back and forth in her cupped hands, crooning to them.

When Christmas came, the first she could really remember, the church placed a life-size crèche at the front of the altar. My daughter was interested in it, but all through Advent, the manger was empty. Jesus would be there on Christmas Day, we promised her.

On Christmas, sure enough, there lay the Baby, tucked snugly in his bed of hay. After church, I was talking with friends when I realized my little girl had disappeared. We found her on her knees by the manger; she looked up at us with shining eyes. "Jesus is a *baby!*" I could hear both joy and awe in her voice.

She had been listening to grownups talk about Jesus off and on all her life. But for the first time, she caught a glimpse of Someone she could understand, Someone small and vulnerable, just like her.

My daughter found in this metaphor something with which she identified, while I find something I lack. For many of us, I suspect, the Christ Child points to an emptiness in our lives. During the centuries when most children died before they were five, no wonder the sacred Baby was beloved by artists and mystics; for them, childhood was a

precious, fragile thing. In today's world, the holy Infant may symbolize something our practical adult world has lost, perhaps our sense of
innocence and wonder. That starlit, haloed Christmas Baby points
toward that which our hearts crave.

In *Surprised by Joy,* C. S. Lewis writes of *Sehnsucht*, a concept he
never quite defines except by illustration. The German word literally
means "longing" or "yearning," and in Lewis's personal theology, this
emotion was what eventually drove him to God. The feeling seems to
be made up of melancholy and wonder, joy and desire. Underlying it
is a sense of isolation from that which is essential to our very being.

The Romantic poets—Wordsworth and Byron, Shelley and
Keats, for instance—connected this sense of yearning to humanity's
exile from nature and the past. Their poetry is full of ceaseless nostal-
gia and aching restlessness for something lost and unattainable. But
for C. S. Lewis, *Sehnsucht* was the golden skein he unwound to lead
him into God's presence.

I suspect our metaphors for God are strong, bright threads in
this skein. I long for a baby—someone else might yearn for a friend or
a lover, a home or achievement. But ultimately, if we each follow these
threads far enough, we may find not the thing we thought we craved
but something far more numinous. Our longings pull us toward God.
The tangible metaphors present in our lives may help us to touch
God's skin, but those that are absent—like childhood's lost innocence—may be even more poignant.

And yet we've tended to relegate the Christ Child to nativity
scenes and children's stories. We assume he's the rosy and simplified
Disney version of the Gospel. He seems too small and helpless to be
relevant to our cruel, grown-up world. His innocence seems naïve.

This year, though, while I was compiling a book of Christmas
poetry, I stumbled on a sixteenth-century poem that spoke of the
Christ Child without the usual sentimental prettiness.

As I in hoary winter's night stood shivering in the snow,
Surprised I was with sudden heat which made my heart to glow;

And lifting up a fearful eye to view what fire was near,
A pretty Babe all burning bright did in the air appear.

. . .

With that he vanished out of sight and swiftly shrunk away,
And straightway I called into mind that it was Christmas Day.

"The Burning Babe" by Robert Southwell has an odd flavor to the modern taste—especially in other stanzas where the newborn Baby speaks first of frying and then melting in a bath of blood. I didn't include the poem in the pretty gift book I was compiling.

Somehow, though, the graphic words have the ring of truth. The story of the Christmas Baby is full of wonder and light—but how relevant is this lovely story in a world where babies are sometimes slaughtered? We cannot escape the Holocaust's terrible truth, and if we could, the more recent events in Bosnia and elsewhere would cast their horrible shadows across that long-ago stable. But that stable was never as sweet and pretty as we have made it over the centuries. The real nativity scene would not have been a glowing place with tidy straw and clean, friendly animals. Instead, Christ's first breaths must have drawn in the odors of excrement and blood. His incarnation as a human baby was joyful and glorious—and it also meant that the divine would now be vulnerable to pain and death and horror.

And yet despite the terrors of our world, regardless of adult weariness or desperation, babies come to us with a message of hope. When I became a mother for the first time, my image of God was radically changed as my own love for my babies taught me of God's love for me. Until recently, I never considered that the opposite was true as well: My babies' love for me taught me just as much.

Young children are such brand-new creatures, full of delight and wonder and curiosity. They do not hide layers of themselves away from sight, like the unseen dangerous bulk of an iceberg beneath the water; instead, they are uncomplicated, without subterfuge, all one shining, visible piece. And most of all, young children love unconditionally, without question or criticism. When I looked into my babies' faces, of course I saw the face of God. How could I help but?

In the same way, God's vast majesty did not speak as clearly to Thérèse of Lisieux as did his *littleness*. Like my youngest daughter kneeling beside the crèche, Thérèse used her sense of her own smallness as the vehicle to identify herself with the Christ Child, and she gave herself to him as his plaything. Her theology may at first glance seem childish and sentimental, but her "little way" to God must be what Christ meant when he told us to become like little children. "You must be born again," the Gospel tells us. Is it saying we must find again our newborn essence? How can we hope to know God unless we too, like him, are as vulnerable, as full of innocence and joy as a baby?

Today, sitting cross-legged under a tree while my two younger children play in the park, I watch a little boy totter toward me. His short, fat legs stumble over nothing and he falls down in a heap. Undisturbed, he rolls onto his back and smiles up at the sky with a chortle of pleasure. When a crow flaps overhead and settles in the tree, the boy struggles up to his feet. "Bood," he says and lays his small hand on my knee while he bends close to my face. He points up at the crow. "Bood." The single earnest word holds a wealth of meaning, depths of wonder and satisfaction, joy and friendliness.

Watching him, I feel the familiar ache inside my chest; I long to sweep this child up and press my face into his warmth, but his mother calls him back to her side. He looks over his shoulder at me one last time, then waves a dimpled fist and dives into his mother's arms. At nearly the same moment, my own two children throw themselves down beside me. As they lean against me, I feel their warmth against my arms. My daughter tells me she's found a grimly-elf in the grass; she's going to take it home with her.

"What's a grimly-elf?" I ask.

"Part unicorn, part lion, part seagull." My son looks up at me from beneath his acorn cap of hair. "They're about six inches long."

He speaks as matter-of-factly as if he were informing me of some well known scientific fact. "They live in the dirt."

My daughter holds up the empty cup of her hands. "He's right here. He's feeling sick."

I look at her face, her brown bright eyes, the nutmeg sprinkle of freckles across her nose, her gap-toothed smile. "Why's he sick?"

"He ate too much dust. I'm going to have to put him on a diet. I'm going to make him a bed in my room." She purses her lips. "I think his name is Albert. Or Elvis."

She puts Albert-Elvis carefully in her T-shirt pocket, then leaps to her feet. Her brother follows her, and I lean back against my tree to watch them play.

I realize then that the divine is revealed not only in the vulnerable newness of an infant or a toddler but also in the ceaseless, creative imagination of an older child. According to author John O'Donohue, "Possibility is the secret heart of creativity"; adults often see only the bland surface of the commonplace, but children perceive possibilities everywhere. They see with God's eyes.

Children are not tiny saints, of course. They may be innocent, joyful, and creative, but they can also be self-centered and demanding; the metaphor only works so far. Adolescents can be particularly trying to adult patience—but still, I find God's image in my adolescent daughter as well.

Caught between childhood and maturity, adolescence is such a painful and glorious time. My oldest daughter can be a sullen, hunched-over bundle of misery one moment—and a blur of grace and laughter the next. Her sense of justice is stern and passionate; like a bright arrow, she targets child labor and prejudice, scornful of society's excuses. I admire her kindness and compassion—and I'm sometimes impatient with the intensity of her emotions.

Today, after my younger children and I returned from the park, I drove my older daughter and a friend to the mall to shop for bathing suits. As I watched them strut and pose and listened to their giggles and chatter, I remembered a novel I read recently by Father Andrew

Greeley. In it, one of his characters compares God to an adolescent girl. "I argue this position," he says,

> based on the observation that no one in our experience is more exuberant, more energetic, more playful, more out-rageous, more fanciful, and more excessive than young women of our species....
>
> How can we avoid the conclusion that Our God is an exuberant and incorrigible show-off? Consider the wild variety of species that inhabit our tiny speck of solar dust. Consider the inordinate and totally unjustified number of solar systems and galaxies, black holes and quarks, protons and weak forces, great attractors and star clusters which constitute our universe as we know it. Who could possibly deny that this display is excessive?
>
> ...How can we possibly deny that this is the kind of fun and games we expect of adolescents and especially adolescent women?...
>
> Metaphors are not strict comparisons. Nonetheless I insist that such behavior, trying as it is to those who must tend to these charming if on occasion feckless creatures, does represent an unpredictable exuberance which may be revelatory...of our ever-youth God, a God for whom it is always spring....

As adults, sometimes we have not only lost our innocence but our exuberance as well. We have forgotten how to play; we no longer remember how to taste life's sweet wildness. If the sight of the Christ Child fills us with yearning, perhaps we are also longing for all that our own hearts have lost.

Many self-help books today speak of the "inner child," that needy child-self we each hide inside our hearts who cries out for atten-tion, who throws tantrums and blinks back tears of hurt. This aspect of our personalities is usually demanding and irrational—but it may also be the part of us that loves to play, that delights in small joys.

Most of us have learned to suppress the hidden children inside us. Like any children, they can be needy and unreasonable. But if we learn to nurture these inner children, to protect and treasure them, might we find that they too give us a glimpse of the divine? We may even find we are sheltering the Christ Child's presence in our lives.

A statue of Anthony of Padua stood in the church we attended when my children were small. My family often took the pew by Anthony's plaster feet; I would glance up at his face while I struggled to keep my kids quiet during the service.

The statue had a narrow, straight nose and a vulnerable mouth that almost smiled. Except for his shaved head and brown robe, he reminded me of my nephew, a gentle young man whose quiet sense of humor endeared him to my kids. Apparently, Anthony was also good with children, for the Child on his book looked relaxed and happy. Anthony's wide dark eyes were fixed on the Child's face.

According to the legend, back in the thirteenth century Anthony was a guest in someone's home. While Anthony was studying in his room, his host became curious about the young monk and spied on him through a crack in the door. To his amazement, he found Anthony holding the Christ Child on his open book with a tender familiarity.

Tonight as I read in the library, I smiled suddenly, struck by the thought of that same Child springing from the page. Perhaps he also jumped into my arms later when I walked home through the woods watching fireflies glimmer in the evening fog...or as I laughed with my husband over our children's grimly-elf. Maybe the divine Child is here right now, as I write these words.

Over and over he leaps into our lives. Warm and vulnerable, he fits himself into the empty spaces of our hearts. And as he is born anew in us, we too become God's holy children, full of energy and creativity, innocence and unstinting love.

And whoso shall receive one such little child in my name receiveth me.

—MATTHEW 18:5 KJV

May the Spirit of God touch you with his essence,
and the Child of eternity be born in you.

—ANGELUS SILESIUS

Friend

Human love and the delights of friendship,
...are to be treasured up as hints of what shall be hereafter.

—BEDE JARRETT

Together we look for the signs of God, the glimpses of grace.
Surely when someone walks with you along the path, looking for
breadcrumbs, it is a magnificent manifestation of a special
kind of friendship: a Trinitarian friendship....

—MADELEINE L'ENGLE

Suppose you are a woman, an ordinary lower-class woman who has made a mistake or two in your life. You know the way the world is; you understand all too well that you are a member of the out-group. You have a hard face, lined with hurt and anger and guilt, and your body is heavy and weary. So when you see a member of the privileged race, a man no less, sitting all alone by the village well one hot summer afternoon, you flick him a wary glance. You know he will not deign to look your way—or if he does, he'll only be interested in using you sexually.

As you drop your bucket into the well, you look at the man out of the corners of your eyes; you can't help but feel a little curious. After all, this stranger is on your territory, not his. Maybe you resent the way he sits so comfortably, so relaxed and at ease; if the tables were turned, and you were the one who had ventured into his community, you would have felt defensive and edgy. But he is clearly comfortable inside

his own skin; obviously, no one has ever taunted him because of its color. No one has ever made him feel he is inferior simply because of his race.

And then the man speaks to you. "Please." His voice is quiet. "Will you give me a drink?" His words startle you so much that your hands slip on the rope, and the bucket splashes back into the water.

"Why are you asking me for a drink?" you blurt. "You know who you are. You know who I am." You hear the bitterness and scorn in your voice.

But then, somehow, you find yourself talking to this quiet stranger. At first glance, the two of you have nothing in common. His background and customs are different from your own; you can't even share the understanding two women sometimes find when they discuss the common experiences of childbirth or love. What's more, he speaks of mysteries, abstract things that make no sense, like living water and eternal life and Spirit. And yet you hear yourself sharing your life with him, spilling your heart into his hands, laughing out loud with him, crying....

Something gleaming and alive within each of you seems to leap across the space that separates you. That something pulls you together, and despite your differences—no, *because* of your differences—it shines even brighter. Against all odds, the two of you meet as equals. You, a Samaritan woman, and this man, this Jesus of Nazareth, have become friends.

—————

I suspect that *recognition* is that strange, shiny something that draws our hearts together in friendship. We look beyond ourselves, across the lonely space that separates us from all others, and we see a piece of ourselves in someone else. Jesus did that when he met the woman at the well—and so did she. God does the same when he looks into human hearts—and so do we when we look back. Unbelievably, God and our hearts are able to meet as equals. As *other* as the divine nature is, we still find our own reflection in its depths.

When we do, we are filled with both surprise and delight. It's a little like listening to a standup comedian: We laugh out loud when we recognize our own lives in the comedian's routine. The same startled recognition sometimes makes me laugh until I cry when I get together with my oldest, closest friends.

Like Narcissus, the young man in Greek mythology who spent his time staring at his reflection, we are fascinated by our own identities. Narcissus's fascination turned into obsession, and we too can become so focused on ourselves that we miss the other's reality. Like most obsessions, though, the initial urge is healthy. As human beings, we all long to catch a glimpse of our own souls.

And yet we never can. It's like trying to twist around to see the spot between my shoulder blades; although that particular piece of skin belongs to me quite intimately, my husband is far more familiar with it than I am. The patch of nerve endings there may send me messages of itches and pains—but I can only snatch a peek at it by holding up a mirror in front of another mirror.

That's what friendship does: It's a reciprocal act of mirroring each other, so we can see ourselves. It shines light on who we are. The experience may sometimes be painful, depending on how receptive we are to the truth. Crusty patches of dirt and disease may be lurking unsuspected in the blind spots friendship reveals. Ultimately, however, friendship's light brings healing and wholeness. Friendship helps us not only recognize our own identity; it also helps us claim that identity.

This shining act of mutual recognition cuts across social conventions and categories, just as it did for the Samaritan woman and Jesus. As John Cassian said, friendship "is what is broken by no chances, what no interval of time or space can sever or destroy, and what even death itself cannot part." Friendship lives in eternity, beyond this world's artificial barriers. In this realm, we can lay aside the social masks, the superficial conventions and half-truths. Here we can learn to be real.

V. Solovyov, author of *The Meaning of Love,* puts it this way:

Having discerned and loved the truth of another, not in the abstract but in the substance…we reveal and make actual our own authentic truth, and our own absolute significance, which consists…in our capacity to live not only in ourselves but in another.

In friendship we do not only recognize aspects of ourselves. We also learn to identify with those who are different. Greed, violence, and oppression are only possible when we fail to see others as beings as real as we are. Friendship transforms the way we look at others. It allows us to see with God's eyes.

The Gospel of the New Testament is embodied by friendship. The faith described by Jesus and Saint Paul cannot be lived alone; its bones and ligaments are relationships with other human beings. In these friendships, Christ's life is again incarnated.

In a book called *Life Together,* the German theologian Dietrich Bonhoeffer asserts that human beings cannot be truly alive if they are dependent only on their own resources. Each of us needs divine nourishment and life—what Bonhoeffer calls the Word—from outside our own boundaries. It comes to us daily and anew, says Bonhoeffer, "bringing redemption, righteousness, innocence, and blessedness," through the mouths of others. As friends, we bring to one another the "divine word of salvation."

We see God through our friends—but they are not signposts merely pointing us toward God. Instead, they are more; they are sacraments. God is present in friendship's words and laughter, love and tears. He speaks to us through our friends' voices.

⌒≈⤞⤝⌒

When I was in fifth grade a new girl moved to our school. Patty had thick pale hair that hung in a ragged fringe over her shoulders, and her glasses were blue and pointed. Her hands fluttered with nervous energy, but she always smiled at me. She was jumpy and anxious, and kind to everyone. She was completely different from anyone I had yet known—and yet I recognized in her something of myself.

Thirty years later I still find that combination of similarities and differences in my friendship with Patty. Over the years, we've shared our thoughts on most everything, from sex to politics, from theology to childrearing. We've confessed our crazy fears and laughed at ourselves; we've cried with each other and prayed for each other and complimented each other's new clothes. Sometimes we talk once a day on the phone; sometimes we talk once a month. Either way, no one has ever understood me better; no one has ever made me laugh more. She shows me God's face.

I imagine that Jesus' relationship with Saint John must have been a little like mine with Patty. The two men had probably known each other since they were children, and the years only deepened and broadened their knowledge of each other. But I also like to imagine the friendship Jesus shared with the two people he met on the road to Emmaus after his resurrection. They walked together, talked, shared a meal—and only then did the two friends recognize him. "Oh," they must have cried, "it's *you!*"

I too have experienced friendship's epiphanies. When I married and moved away from my home and friends, I thought I had used up my life's quota of friends; years went by without my making a new friend. Then suddenly new friends leapt into my life from all directions. One of these, a woman named Donna, I had met long ago, but she was simply a pleasant face I ran into at the grocery store or the post office. We chatted about children and church; eventually we discovered we shared career ambitions. A couple of years ago I thought of Donna when I needed to hire another assistant for my work; we worked together pleasantly, never talking about anything deeper than the tasks we shared. And then one night we each took a risk and revealed pieces of our hearts we normally kept hidden. When we did, we discovered we had more in common than we had ever expected, "Oh," I thought, startled and delighted, "it's *you!*" I had never guessed—and yet here she was, a person I recognized suddenly as a friend, just as the two disciples on the road to Emmaus finally recognized Jesus.

If I were to continue my list of friends, it would include old friends and new, my sister and my husband, even my children. Friendship lies like a sweet, green kernel contained in all other healthy relationships, a seed that grows as it enriches human interaction. *Webster's* tells me our word *friend* comes from Old English roots that meant both to love and to free—and that is what friendship does: It ties us together with love even while it frees us to be uniquely ourselves. Each friendship reveals yet one more facet of God, the eternal Other.

A few years ago, I sat in an adult Sunday school class and listened while the pastor lectured on the Trinity. The three-person God, the pastor claimed, is a hierarchy: God the Creator is at the top of this triad; beneath him, is God the incarnate Redeemer; and at the bottom is God the Spirit. The pastor's views disturbed me. I am only an amateur theologian, so I did not know how to contradict his position intelligently, but the notion of hierarchy seems alien to my concept of the Gospel. If the divine reaches out to creation in friendship, then certainly the Trinity itself must be a friendship, the template for all other relationships of equality and love.

The long-ago Christian Celts were fascinated by the Trinity. One of their ancient prayers is the Breastplate of Saint Patrick, which contains these lines:

I arise today
Through a mighty strength, the invocation of the Trinity,
Through belief in the threeness,
Through confession of the oneness,
Of the Creator of Creation.

The Celts understood the "mighty strength" that's found in the unity of separate equals.

"I no longer call you servants," Jesus told his disciples (John 15:15 NIV). "Instead, I have called you friends." In other words, Jesus was not communicating with his disciples as a superior does with his inferiors; now, Jesus was talking to them as equals, as friends.

Friendship is killed by feelings of superiority or possessiveness, by the assumption that the other's reality is not as real as our own, that the other exists merely for our own benefit. Along similar lines, in his book *Intimacy,* Henri Nouwen writes that a mature faith recognizes that the divine exists outside of our minds; its reality is not dependent on our own. "Our religious sentiment will never be mature," Nouwen says, "(1) if God is not the Other, (2) if prayer is not a dialogue, and (3) if religion is not a source of creative autonomy." These three conditions are also necessary for any healthy friendship.

Christian theology upholds the paradox that God is both transcendent and immanent. I suspect that's just another way of saying that, like all good friends, God is both separate and yet one with us. God is no imaginary friend we can control and manipulate; his reality is startling and sometimes difficult. And yet in God, we recognize the reflection of our truest identities—and when God looks back at us, he sees in us a piece of himself, what the Quakers call "that of God." In friendship, the divine gives itself to us in love, just as Jesus gave himself to the woman at the well. Then, like the Samaritan woman, we too are freed to be ourselves.

With so good a Friend...ever present,
Himself the first to suffer, everything can be borne.
He helps, He strengthens, He never fails, He is the true Friend.

TERESA OF AVILA

Love Him, and keep Him for thy Friend, who when all go away,
will not forsake thee, nor suffer thee to perish at the last.

THOMAS Á KEMPIS

7

Bridegroom and Lover

*O my beloved Christ, crucified by love, I wish to be
a bride for your Heart....*

—ELIZABETH OF THE TRINITY

*As a bridegroom rejoices over his bride,
so will your God rejoice over you.*

—ISAIAH 62:5

The summer before we were married, my husband Paul and I were
apart for six weeks. He was in New York City, giving psychological
tests to children, and I was in western New York State, eight hours
away, teaching summer school. We were both saving up money for our
honeymoon. Our jobs would keep us apart until two days before our
wedding.

I thought the summer would never end. During the day I stayed
busy, teaching and preparing for the wedding—but at night, I lay
awake hour after hour, filled with frustrated longing. I wanted Paul. I
wanted to see him and talk with him face to face; I wanted to touch
him and feel him and smell him. I wanted to make love with him.
And the summer was so slow and endless, that I thought my longing
would never be fulfilled.

When we talked on the phone, we argued. Of course, we had
also argued when we were together, but then it had been easier to
laugh and kiss and let our pleasure in each other overwhelm our differences. Paul's disembodied voice filled me with yearning—but it

also made me edgy with frustration. I resented the power he had over my life.

And yet somehow, away from him, longing for him, his image grew sharper and clearer in my mind. The fan would drone endlessly in the window of my attic apartment, and the sheets were heavy and damp with sweat; I would lie awake picturing the smooth skin of Paul's big hands, or his lower lip, or the way his T-shirts always smelled of bleach and cotton. When we were together, I was often distracted by my own reactions to the moment, but away from him, I analyzed his emotions, I considered his ideas, and I put myself in his position. I tried to imagine what it would be like to *be* him, this other person who had become so important to me.

The experience wasn't always pleasant. Frequently, I was terrified. I felt cross and anxious and resentful. *You're asking too much of me,* I wanted to say. *I don't want to accommodate you in my world. I was doing quite nicely without you.*

I remembered my old fantasies that had once lulled me to sleep when I was younger, long, involved romances about dark, scowling men who were madly in love with me. Paul's face was not stern and chiseled like theirs, no muscle ever ticked dangerously in his cheek at the thought of losing me, nor was he prone to giving me sardonic, wolfish smiles. Instead, he was like no man I had ever imagined; his face and his personality both were full of unexpected quirks. Loving him seemed like the most natural thing I'd ever done—and at the same time it was like nothing I had ever done before. I felt as though my longing for him had turned me into someone new, someone entirely different from the person I had always been.

I've never done well with delayed gratification; I began to wonder if we would ever see each other again. I was gripped with a terrible fear that some awful tragedy would strike...we would never have the chance to live together and fulfill our love.

And then at last the long summer came to an end. We saw each other a day earlier than we had planned, because the father of a close friend was dying. I met Paul's eyes with the sound of a respirator in the background, and then, half-ashamed, we found a custodian's closet to hide in and fell against each other. Death was just down the hallway—but Paul was here at last, beneath my hands, against my face, warm and breathing and *real*. And he was just as desperate as I was. We seemed each to be trying to suck the other in, pressing as close as skin and lips would allow.

⚬

I am like one crazed and transformed by my hunger for you.

According to Catherine of Siena, these are the words that Jesus says to us. Again and again, she refers to God as "madly in love with your creature," "like one drunk with love." God, says Catherine, is as hungry for our presence as a frustrated lover. What a strange thought: Just as I yearned for Paul that summer before our wedding, God yearns for me.

Bernard of Clairvaux was the first to write about God in sexual terms. His bridal mysticism became all the rage (with mystics) during the Middle Ages; obviously, this was an image that spoke loudly to those medieval theologians, men and women alike. Celibate themselves, the bridegroom metaphor made sense to them. It helped them visualize the unimaginable. Freud might say that their repressed sexuality was merely surfacing somewhere else, but you can look at it from a slightly different angle: Maybe they put their sexual energy to practical use, allowing it to be the tangible vehicle that carried them toward God.

That summer before my wedding, I doubt it ever occurred to me to look for God in the midst of my sexual longing; after all, we seldom classify frustration as a particularly "holy" emotion. But looking back, I catch sight of something new, as though strange and beautiful eyes are looking back at me from a familiar face.

Bernard of Clairvaux wasn't the first to have a vision of that same passionate face I glimpse today. As early as the second century, Origen wrote that an ardent love for the Bridegroom—for Christ— was necessary for complete union with God. And both Origen and

122

Bernard drew their inspiration from the Bible itself. In the Book of Revelation, John writes that Christ calls his people his Bride (Rev 21:2), and in the Gospels, Jesus identifies himself as the Bridegroom (Matt 25; John 3:29). These Scripture references speak of joy and fulfillment but they are not particularly sexual; both John and Christ, however, would surely have been familiar with the Old Testament book that was the origin of this metaphor: the Song of Songs, the most erotic of all Bible books.

The Song of Songs is openly and joyously sexual. Oddly enough, nowhere in its eight chapters does it even mention God; it never explicitly states that the lovers are metaphors for God and his people. Instead, the book breathes sensuality; as I read it, I can practically smell the pheromones in the air. The lovers delight in each other's taste and touch (2:3; 7:6–11), smell and voice (1:12–14; 2:8); they praise each other's body (4:1–7; 6:4–10), and they compare each other to food and animals, fruits and flowers. And somehow in the midst of all this unabashed eroticism, humanity has never failed to find an image of both God's love for us, and ours for him.

Anything that is sacramental is two things at once. The Eucharist is both bread and wine *and* the body and blood of Christ. And in the Song of Songs I read that sex *is* sex—a physical delight and a joyful expression of human love—*and* it is something more, something that reveals God's love for us.

Just as I longed for Paul before our marriage, some days I long for God. I am no medieval mystic, delighting in pain and suffering; my yearning tends to make me frustrated and resentful. Wanting something so badly, something that lies utterly beyond my ability to control, threatens my own sense of power. It scares me. And I am apt to begin to wonder if I will ever find fulfillment, if my yearning is not doomed from the very beginning. But I have felt all these things before, with Paul. And I remember how sweet our wedding day was, how sweeter still our wedding night. They were worth the wait.

I also remember the desperate hunger in our hands and lips and bodies. God loves me like *that?* If this metaphor is a window into

123

God's heart, then the glimpse I get is both unfamiliar and lovely—and nearly overwhelming.

In the end, what this all means is this: When I relate to God, my "spirit" and my body are not two separate things, any more than they are when I relate to a human lover. The medieval mystics knew this. Angela of Foligno wrote that Christ said to her, "My beloved and my bride, love thou Me! All thy life, thy eating and drinking and sleeping and all that thou dost is pleasing unto Me, if only thou lovest Me....I desire that in this world thou shouldst hunger and long after Me and shouldst ever be eager to find Me." Clearly, Angela was speaking of the same sweet, yearning love, a love that is expressed in the physical world, that I felt for Paul.

All too often I'm still trapped by the Greek dualism that splits our body and soul into two neat pieces. But if Christ is my lover, my bridegroom, then the intangible is rooted in the tangible. The concrete draws meaning from that which I can never touch with my fingers.

Behold, the bridegroom cometh; go ye out to meet him.

—MATTHEW 25:6 KJV

*All of our interior, spiritual seeking, whether in grace or in glory,
and all of our going out through the practice of virtue in various
exercises are all for the purpose of meeting and being united
with Christ our Bridegroom, for he is our eternal rest
and the goal and reward of all our activity.*

—JAN VAN RUUSBROEC

Lord, you are my lover, the object of my desire.

—MECHTILD OF MAGDEBURG

8
Spouse

No longer will they call you Deserted or name your land Desolate.
But you will be called...Beulah, for the Lord will take delight in you,
and your land will be married.

—ISAIAH 62:4

What joy it must be when God espouses his fiancée
In his eternal Word, through his Spirit!

—ANGELUS SILESIUS

When I was a romantic young woman, I was fascinated for a while by the Middle Ages' concept of courtly, idealized love: *l'amour courtois*, a lavish and noble sacrifice of self. At the time, I imagined myself to be in love with a man who had broken my heart; although he clearly wanted nothing more to do with me, I continued to think of him endlessly. Every day I took long walks alone, my head filled with fantasies of heroic, undying passion. The man who obsessed me might never return my love, I eventually acknowledged, but I vowed to give my wounded heart to Christ instead.

I shake my head now at the memory, but I was an unusually naïve and inexperienced young woman, and this was my first taste of love. I threw my new wealth of extravagant emotion at Christ, my Lover-Bridegroom who would always love me and long only for my happiness, who would approve of me and never hurt me. At night, I read my old literature books from college and memorized these words:

Spouse

Love service is the essential expression of *amour courtois*. In contrast to blind and transient passion, *amour fol*, courtly love was conceived as *amour voulu*, an unchanging disposition of the individual will.

Reading this now, the words still have meaning to me, I find, but they call to mind something far more prosaic and familiar, like some well-used household item, rather than the rare and lovely fantasy I conjured up when I was younger. Nearly two decades later, long married now, I seldom think of God as my Lover or Bridegroom. I no longer fling my bundle of frustrated longing at God's feet. Instead, I am physically satisfied and complacently mated. My husband makes me laugh, makes me scream, fights with me, makes love with me— but only rarely does he fill me with the aching longing he did that summer we spent apart before our marriage. Seldom do I feel for him anything that could be equated with the constant, helpless yearning— C. S. Lewis's *Sehnsucht*—that I feel for a God I cannot see or touch.

The prophet Isaiah speaks of delight in the same breath he calls Israel Beulah ("married")—but still, Beulah is such a prosaic-sounding name. It brings to my mind images of a sturdy, matter-of-fact woman with her sleeves rolled up to clean the toilet. I'm afraid other metaphors speak more sharply to me now. After all, I am no radiant, young bride anymore—and my husband no longer shines with the bridegroom's new splendor. He is no stranger to me, this man with whom I live and sleep, raise children and keep house, argue and pay bills. Ours is an *amour voulu,* an unchanging disposition of our individual wills, but our love wears ordinary clothes rather than romance's exotic finery.

The relationship I lack may be the metaphor that calls to me most loudly with God's voice. Maybe God reaches to me through the holes in my life, the empty gaps where I stand shivering and alone, acknowledging my need. And maybe I see my husband as all too human to be a metaphor for the God who loves perfectly and endlessly.

127

The last few days, for instance, my husband and I have struggled and pushed against each other, snapping and sniping, grappling for our own space, our own way. Tethered by love and promises, we twist and pull in frustration and anger and hurt feelings. Obviously, our marriage is not a good metaphor for a God of peace and joy.

And yet lying in bed last night, a chilly ten inches of sheet separating us, our hands slid together simultaneously through the darkness. A moment before I'd been lying prim and straight, my own two cold hands fitted neatly together, left with right, like two halves of a clamshell. But then he pulled me closer, his fingers warm and uncomfortably wide between mine. I ran my thumb back and forth against his skin, and I was struck by his strangeness, his sheer *otherness*. I felt his pulse beneath my fingers; but I will never hear the silent working of his brain.

Maybe I dreamed once of a lover who would always stroke and approve and long only for my happiness—but a lover like that would have only been an extension of myself, not a separate entity in his own right. It would have been like my own two hands clasping each other, fitting perfectly together. But my husband will never be me. As much as we love each other, we will always fight each other for space and power.

God does call me through the hungry, lonely holes in my heart. But the danger of seeing God only as the thing I lack is that I tend to romanticize what I don't have—and that very air of exotic fantasy distances me from God. I cannot touch God's face or feel his hand or smell his skin; his absence from my life fills me with a lover's bittersweet yearning. But at the same time, the Bible implies that God is both near and far away (Jer 23:23), intimately present even when he is absent—another of the many paradoxes that are woven through faith's fabric.

Like Jacob with the angel, my husband and I contend with each other. We struggle and refuse to let go; and I emerge both wounded and blessed, limping forward with a new identity that enlarges my sense of who I am. Don't biblical scholars agree that Jacob's angel was a manifestation of God—the divine with skin on?

In the dark last night, I drifted toward sleep, my hand still gripped by this familiar stranger, my worst enemy and best friend, my lover and husband. Beside me, I felt his muscles jump, jerking him awake. "What?" he grunted. "Did you say something?"

"I don't think so." Silly and sleepy, I let out a snort of laughter. "But you can call me Beulah."

"Sure." He didn't have a clue what I was talking about, and he didn't care. He just wanted to go back to sleep.

His grip on my hand tightened, and I winced a little as my wedding ring pressed into my skin. I didn't move away, though. Our three children lay sleeping in their rooms down the hall; I listened to our old house settling in the darkness; I thought about my work waiting for me in the morning. I like this life Paul and I have built together, and my hand in his felt warm and safe.

"Night, Beulah," he murmured and started to snore.

Being married is very different from merely being in love. There's less day-to-day excitement, less agonized yearning, more ordinary life. I suppose it's a little like the difference between bread and cake; I've experienced my share of cake addiction, I must confess, but lately I've come to appreciate bread. After all, it's one of the things that gives me daily strength.

Teresa of Avila speaks of "spiritual betrothal" as the sixth mansion of her "interior castle," while "spiritual marriage" is the seventh mansion. They are two separate things. During spiritual betrothal, she says, we experience intense longing for God, but once we are "married," "the soul always remains with God in that center." In other words, marriage opens a door into an entirely new place to live. John of the Cross writes of spiritual marriage as a "lived union with God in Jesus"; because of this union, we enter the house where the Trinity lives. We become one with the God whose very essence is made up of relationship.

In my experience, relationships are messy things—and my marriage is probably the messiest relationship I have. Unlike a lover, my husband impinges on my life in all sorts of awkward ways; he tangles my emotions into knots; his life presses so close to mine that I can rarely manage to bring our relationship into objective focus. When he was merely my lover, on the other hand, he was far enough away that I could step back and admire his entire person, as though he were Michelangelo's *David* standing at a distance on a pedestal. Back then, Paul didn't crowd so close that I ended up with a blurry, Picasso-like picture of jumbled eyes and nose and mouth. A lover's image tends to be more classically beautiful, I think, but these days my husband refuses to stand still long enough for me to draw his outline with neat and pretty strokes. He won't stand primly on his pedestal.

I wouldn't really want him to. My marriage, this demanding, often chaotic relationship, gives me something far beyond a static image of God. Marriage is not simply about the fulfillment of my desires; instead, it is a relationship that fertilizes my identity with life. The process is muddy and haphazard, sometimes painful, and always beyond my ability to control. But rooted in the ordinary, daily soil of commitment, I am free to grow and be fruitful.

⸙

The words I've used to describe marriage are the sorts of things I take for granted: bread, a home, the earth itself. So long as I am not deprived of them, they drop into the background of my existence; and yet they are essential to my life's daily, detailed drama. Like my marriage, my relation to God nourishes me and shelters me. It gives me stability and feeds the many branches of my life.

Author John O'Donohue writes that when two people marry, "each comes out of the loneliness of exile, home to the one house of belonging…." In God, as in my marriage, I find my own "house of belonging." In both relationships, I am made comfortable and safe.

Secure that I am loved, I find the courage to try new things, to venture to new heights.

Neither relationship is easy, though. No matter how intimate the union I share with my husband—or with God—at the same time, the distance between us is still an unbridgeable gap, a chasm I will never cross, at least in this life. Both relationships wound my selfish ego. And both challenge me to become more than I have ever been.

The Sacred Person of the Divine Word revealed to me that
he was in truth the spouse of the faithful soul.
...At that moment, this adorable Person seized my soul and embracing it
with indescribable love, united it to himself, taking it as his spouse.

—MARIE OF THE INCARNATION

In this very deep encounter, this very intimate and ardent approach, each
spirit (ours and that of God himself) is wounded by love....their faces
are thus mutually revealed. As a result, the two try to outdo each
other in love. Each asks for what the other is and,
in turn, offers him what he himself is.

—JAN VAN RUUSBROEC

Lord, love me passionately, love me often, love me long.
The more passionately you love me, the more beautiful I become.
The more often you love me, the purer I become.
The longer you love me, the holier I become.

—MECHTILD OF MAGDEBURG

9

Self and Soul

We read that our Lord said: "Let us make human beings in our own image" (Gen 1:26). And that is what he did. So like to himself did he make the soul of a person that neither in the kingdom of heaven nor on earth among all the splendid creatures that God created in such a wonderful way is there any creature that resembles him as much as does the soul of a human being.

—MEISTER ECKHART

The center of the soul is God.
When the soul loves and understands and enjoys God to its utmost capacity it will have reached its deep centre, God....
The love of God will be able to wound the soul at its deepest point; that is it is brought to the state where it appears to be God himself.

—JOHN OF THE CROSS

As a child, I never would have dreamed that my own soul might be a metaphor for God. When I looked into the murky depths inside me, I caught no glimpses of the divine; instead I often felt a sense of shame and despair. If I could, I would have rid myself of my own heart.

In Sunday school we sang the words, "My heart was black with sin, Until the Savior came in." I knew that Jesus wanted to live in my heart—but I assumed he would need to scour it clean and empty before he could make room for himself. I understood conversion to mean that God came to live inside me; I imagined this concept, however, as God occupying the hollow shell of my being. The need I felt

133

to vacate my own self filled me with both frustration and resentment; I was certain God would never live inside me. How could he when I was so crowded with myself?

Today, I may see things a little differently, but I am still often confused by this metaphor for the divine. I see God easily in the elements of nature; I sense his presence as well in human relationships. But how can I touch him in my own soul? The very idea seems selfish and conceited.

I don't think I'm alone in these feelings. Our culture is conflicted when it comes to thinking of our own selves. On the one hand, we are constantly preoccupied with our personal interests and needs; we seek self-expression, self-esteem, and self-achievement as values in our lives. But on the other hand, we feel guilty that we are not more concerned for others; with shame, we try to disguise our selfishness, self-centeredness, and self-aggrandizement.

Few of us have healthy and holy paradigms for thinking of the self. We look for God's presence in others, but we blush to think we might catch a glimpse of him within our own identities. We are like the peasants in this story from Indian literature:

> A group of six peasants forded a river. Afterward, concerned that someone might have been lost, the leader counted the group: one, two, three, four, five. Having omitted himself from the count, he assumed that someone was lost. Each of the other peasants then counted for themselves: one, two, three, four, five. Since none of them remembered to count themselves, they were dismayed: someone was clearly lost in the river. The six peasants spent many sad and desperate hours searching the river for the missing person. Then someone else came along and asked them about their dilemma. "You are forgetting to count yourselves!" he told them. The six peasants were overjoyed to find that no one was missing after all, and they all proceeded on their way.

Like the peasants, we can count the ways we find the divine presence in others, but we fail to include ourselves in this spiritual tally. Sad and desperate because we believe God is somehow missing from our lives, we search for his presence everywhere but in ourselves. The six peasants may seem foolish to us, and yet our sense of false modesty and shame makes us as silly.

To use yet another story as an illustration, those of us who want to be perceived as Christians are often like the naked emperor pretending to be dressed in new clothes—except in our case, we are trying to cover our naked selves with the trappings of godliness so that when others look at us they will see only God's presence. Of course we fool no one except ourselves. And all along, God only wants to show himself to the world through the vehicle of our individual and quirky souls. If others will see him there, then surely we too could glimpse his face hidden in our own.

It's no wonder we get confused, though. After all, we have no clear definition of what exactly a soul or a self is.

For centuries, philosophers, psychologists, and scientists have been trying to define and map human consciousness. Early in the twentieth century, Freud broke the self into three parts: the ego, the superego, and the id. His concept of the ego, the personality's organizing point, continues to influence our thinking today. But other modern thinkers have rejected that the soul or the self exists at all; it is merely the "ghost in the machine," a vague, unproven concept we have attached to our biological brains, nothing more than an illusion. But if self is merely an illusion, who is having the illusion?

The early Greeks were some of the first thinkers to try to explain this apparently self-evident and yet ultimately unknowable concept. Plato said the human soul was the part of a person that most resembled the divine, since it was invisible, immortal, and wise. Plutarch built on this thinking a bit more and developed the concept of the *dae-mon*—a sort of guardian spirit given to us by God, part of us and yet separate; Plutarch defined the daemon as our intellect, the piece of the divine being that dwells within each of us.

In author Philip Pullman's fantasy world, human beings have visible daemons, parts of their own selves appearing in animal form. Each person's daemon is her closest companion, her deepest friend, while also being an expression of her inmost identity. The daemon is the embodiment of the individual's creativity, courage, and insight. Daemon and human are one being, and yet they love and care for each other with tenderness and loyalty. If our real-life world had visible daemons like this, I suspect many of them would appear to be neglected and starved—or lazy and apathetic. Our modern-day schematics for the self offer us no similar way to appreciate and care for that which is finest in our own beings. If we did, we might find that as we nurtured our daemons, those valiant creative aspects of our own souls, we would also touch God's skin.

The Greek philosopher Philo, however, was not as concerned with daemons as he was with defining the parts of the self. Like modern psychologists, he sought to map the various aspects of human identity, and to do so, he separated the soul (the *psyche*, our emotions) from the mind (the *nous*). The mind, said Philo, is what most resembles God—and because it resembles God, it yearns for him. It is the part of each of us that is constantly pointed toward God like an arrow.

We may define the mind differently today, but twentieth-century Russian Orthodox monk Anthony Bloom nevertheless echoes Philo's thoughts; "God reveals himself to us," Bloom writes, "in this awareness that we are essentially a cry for him." Our need is the starting point for our recognition of the divine presence in our own souls. And yet we know all too well the ways we are separated from God. With so many yawning chasms between us and God—so much sin—how can we find the divine image in ourselves? Surely our desperate need alone is not enough.

For the Greek philosophers, however, our need for the divine pointed toward our actual destiny; the need would not be there if it were not destined to one day be fulfilled. The concept of *telos* or destiny was essential to these Greeks' definition of human identity. We see destiny as something that lies in the future, distant from the present moment, but the Greeks saw no such distinction. Despite the fluctuations of temporal circumstances, what we are meant to be, that which we *will* be, defines our being eternally.

Twentieth-century psychologist Carl Jung agreed that the self simultaneously contains both the quest for divine reality and the realization. According to Jung, in the first half of life the self is like an external envelope that contains our personalities—but in the second half of life, ideally at least, the self becomes an inward locus of balance and harmony. The self, Jung believed, now is equivalent to the presence of Christ.

But obviously not everyone automatically achieves this divine sense of balance and harmony. Psychologists like Abraham Maslow, Carl Rogers, and Alfred Adler acknowledged that not everyone reaches this goal, but they still defined it as an ideal milestone in human development; they referred to this concept of internal harmony as "self-actualization" or the development of the "creative self."

The term "self-actualization" always makes me think of the children's story *The Velveteen Rabbit*. The stuffed rabbit in the story wanted desperately to become "real," just as some part of each of us longs to achieve "actualization." When our selves are real, then the divine presence will be revealed in our identities.

This may be the ultimate destiny of each of us—but how can we achieve this milestone in the here and now? The Greek philosopher Plotinos recognized the paradox between our sin and the eternal presence of God in our hearts when he wrote: "The soul is without light when not contemplating the One....This is the veritable *telos* [destiny] of the soul, to lay hold of that light, not through another light, but by itself, through which it sees....How, then, might this happen? Abandon all else."

More than a millennium later, Christian mystic Meister Eckhart repeats Plotinos's words:

Make a start with yourself, and abandon yourself....People who seek [the divine presence] in external things—be it in places or ways of life or people or activities or solitude or poverty or degradation—however great such a thing may be or whatever it may be, still it is nothing....People who seek in this way are doing it all wrong; the further they wander, the less they find what they are seeking. They go around like someone who has lost his way; the further he goes, the more lost he is. Then what ought he to do? He ought to begin by forsaking himself, because then he has forsaken everything. Truly, if a man renounced a kingdom or the whole world but held on to himself, he would not have renounced anything.

"We must renounce [the self], and sacrifice all self-interest," affirms Fénelon in the seventeenth century, and down through the centuries mystics have repeated this same thought again and again. The Apostle Paul may have been the one to begin it all; "I have been crucified with Christ and I no longer live, but Christ lives in me," he wrote in his letter to the Galatians (2:20).

These thoughts seem to bring me back full circle to where I began as a child. Must I reject my own identity before the divine image can be seen in me? Perhaps the difficulty lies in our vocabulary, our inability to define the various aspects of our nature. Psychologist Erich Fromm differentiated between selfishness and genuine self-love; they are actually opposites, he wrote, for the selfish person hates himself, while self-love and love for others are bound together. Fromm pointed out that Jesus spoke of loving our neighbors as ourselves, implying that we can truly care for others only if we care for ourselves, and vice versa.

Mother Teresa, who gave her own life away so selflessly to the poor of India, would have agreed with Fromm. "The Word becomes flesh in us," she wrote, "when we give that Word away to others....In loving and serving, we prove that we have been created in the likeness of God, for God is love and when we love we are like God." Yes, the selfish ego must die. We must give away everything we are, abandon the whole selfish package of worries and wants. Like the Velveteen Rabbit, we must allow ourselves to be erased by love—so that we can become the creatures we have always longed to be. When that happens, we are free to love ourselves at last. Now we can care for own being and appreciate the gifts we find there. Now we can finally see the image of God in our own hearts.

❦

Jesus loved to talk in paradoxes. "Whoever tries to keep his life will lose it," he said, "and whoever loses his life will preserve it" (Luke 17:33). Jesus also said that unless a grain of wheat falls into the earth and dies, it can never grow and yield fruit. The divine image, the germ of God's presence, lives in each of us.

God does not want the empty shell of my life, as I imagined when I was young. Instead, it is the other way around: The empty husk has no value in God's eyes—but when I allow it to be broken, God is revealed as the true seed within. I am reminded of *atman,* the Hindu concept for the supreme universal self, that which is also the innermost essence of each individual. According to the Chandogya Upanishad, atman "dwells in the heart, is smaller than a grain of barley, smaller than a grain of mustard, smaller than a grain of millet, smaller than the germ which is the grain of millet...and yet greater than the earth, greater than the atmosphere, greater than the sky, greater than all the worlds together." No wonder this tiny seed in my own heart is more immense than the entire universe; it is actually God's presence in me.

Empty yourself of everything—and you will be more full than the sky. Abandon yourself—and you will finally become real and whole. Die to yourself—and you will be born.

"You must be born again," Jesus told Nicodemus in the Gospel of John (ch. 3). Nicodemus was a wealthy man, and Jesus seems to be saying to him, "Stop depending on possessions and prestige for your identity. Let go of all that. Let that false self be smashed, so that your true self—the self I created in my own image, the self I am calling you to be for all eternity—can be revealed."

Meister Eckhart writes of spiritual rebirth as a breakthrough, a lightning flash or a sudden eruption of the divine into our own being. Like any birth, it is violent and sometimes painful, and yet it brings new life and great joy. This ongoing birth, a birth that takes place moment by moment, should be the focus of our lives.

In the end, our own soul as a metaphor for the divine becomes the deepest and the most challenging of all. The "spark of the soul," writes Eckhart, "is where the Son is born." As our identities are born anew, so is God's image in our lives. And as we give ourselves away in love, we can celebrate the daily birthdays we share with him.

God is hidden within the soul, and the true contemplative will seek him there in love. O soul, most beautiful of creatures, who ardently longs to know the place where your Beloved is that you may seek him and be united to him. You yourself are the true tabernacle where he dwells, the secret room where he is hidden....To speak more accurately..., "the Kingdom of God is within you." *Courage then, O soul most beautiful! You now know that your Beloved dwells hidden within your own breast. Endeavor therefore to be truly hidden with him.*

—JOHN OF THE CROSS

We must seek for God in us and ourselves in God. This is a work of meditation which we should engage in every day all through our lives.

—ANTHONY BLOOM

God says: Be like Me!

—RABBI MEIR

Conclusion

The idol-maker may know, more or less clearly, that he is only giving
shape to the half-formed concept of God in his head;
that his images are solid metaphors....
Yet the idolater will persist in losing sight of the forest for the trees,
and the god for the image....
Worse yet, the god confined in an image is a shrunken and powerless god.

—JOY DAVIDMAN

Whenever someone recognizes something in God and puts a name on it,
then it is not God....
The idea of God can become the final obstacle to God.

—MEISTER ECKHART

If you meet the Buddha on the road, kill him.

I don't pretend to completely understand this Buddhist koan,
but it always reminds me of one of author Charles Williams's favorite
sayings: "This too is Thou, Lord. Neither is this Thou." In other
words, as soon as a metaphor helps me catch a glimpse of God—
quick! smash it! God cannot be contained by any metaphor. If I try, I
end up with something small and finite and dead. Better to kill it than
to fall down and worship it.

As so much does in the Gospel, it all comes back to paradox.
Pascal says in his *Pensées* that the very things that "reveal" God—
nature, humanity, the Eucharist—are also veils that cover God from

our sight. God shows himself to me in the world I see and touch—and he also hides himself there.

When the Apostle Peter witnessed God revealed in Christ at the transfiguration, he blurted out, "Let's build three shelters here—one for you, one for Moses, and one for Elijah" (Matt 17:4). It's the sort of silly thing I might say (and then I'd lie awake and squirm every time I remembered my words). Maybe Moses and Elijah had nothing better to do than hang around in a little booth, but Peter *knew* Jesus; why would Peter think that Jesus, an active living person, would want to confine himself to a shrine?

But in my own way, I too am tempted to put up shelters around my visions of God. I don't want to just touch God; I want to grab hold of him and keep him handy. I want to define him, make him manageable, make him mine. And yet he continues to elude me.

Gregory of Nyssa wrote that the truest vision of God is this: "never to be satisfied in our desire to see him." Gregory goes on to say,

> Hope always draws the soul from the beauty which is seen to what is beyond, always kindles the desire for the hidden through what is constantly perceived. Therefore, the ardent lover of beauty, although receiving what is always visible as an image of what he desires, yet longs to be filled with the very stamp of the archetype.

God's stamp is on the world around me. He fills my empty heart with everything I touch and see and love. And yet he calls me to come still further, still deeper.

I remember playing hide-and-seek on summer nights when I was very young. As the youngest in the family, I wasn't much good at the game, because I could never quite grasp what I was supposed to do when I was It. My confusion didn't dim the game's magic, though. The soft, warm darkness smelled like grass and earth, and fireflies glimmered first here and then there across the wide lawn. All around me I heard the whispers of the people I loved most; shadows dashed and darted; my outstretched hands skimmed a bare arm, a cotton shirt, a wisp of hair.

Sometimes, I pelted after a dark shape, laughing out loud with triumph. Other times I ran back and forth, calling out with frustration. But once in a while I just stood still, waiting in the darkness. I knew sooner or later, if I waited long enough, loving arms would swoop me close to warm, familiar skin.

The spiritual journey...seems to be a dance between knowing and not knowing, between believing and wondering.

—SCOTT LONDON

Take not, Oh Lord, our literal sense. Lord, in Thy great Unbroken speech our limping metaphor translate.

—C. S. LEWIS

What will it be like when we enjoy a never-ending Communion in the mansion of the King of Heaven?
Then our delight will be without end and without shadow;...
Then we shall no longer see Him veiled beneath the appearance of a baby or a piece of bread,
but in the full light of His infinite splendour.

—THÉRÈSE OF LISIEUX

Reference Notes

Introduction

The first opening quote is from Martin Luther King, Jr., A *Knock at Midnight*, Clayborne Carson and Peter Holloran, eds. (New York: Warner Books, 1998), page 139. The second opening quote is from C. S. Lewis, *The Great Divorce* (New York: Macmillan, 1976), page 129. The quote from *Pilgrim's Regress* by C. S. Lewis (Glasgow, Great Britain: Collins, 1978) is found on pages 219–20. The Carl Jung quote is on page 4 of *Man and His Symbols* (New York: Dell, 1972). I can't be too precise about the Coleridge quote; I found it in a notebook from one of my college literature courses. The similar quote from Gregory Palamas is in *Light from Light,* Louis Dupré and James A. Wiseman, eds. (Mahwah, N.J.: Paulist Press, 1988) on page 199, while Madeleine L'Engle speaks of golden calves versus open doors to God on page 16 of *Penguins and Golden Calves* (Wheaton, Ill.: Shaw, 1996). Paulist Press has a good edition of Julian of Norwich's *Showings*. I believe C. S. Lewis calls God an iconoclast in *Prayer: Letters to Malcolm,* but I haven't been able to track down the exact reference. The closing quote by Dorothy Sayers is on page 22 of *The Mind of the Maker* (New York: Harcourt, Brace, 1941).

Metaphors from the Natural World

1
Rock

The closing quote by Mechtild of Magdeburg I found in *Swallow's Nest*, edited by Marchiene Vroon Rienstra (Grand Rapids, Mich.: Eerdmans, 1992), page 108.

2
Wind

The opening quote by Origen I found in *Light from Light*, page 43. The passages from Genesis are from volume 1 of the Schocken Bible, *The Five Books of Moses*, translated by Everett Fox (New York: Schocken Books, 1995). The passage from 1 Timothy is from the Amplified Bible (Grand Rapids, Mich.: Zondervan, 1976). The quotation from Meister Eckhart and the commentary by Matthew Fox are also from *Light from Light*. The quotations by A. W. Tozer are from *The Pursuit of God*, first published in 1948; a modern edition is available from Christian Publications. A nice illustrated edition of George MacDonald's *At the Back of the North Wind* is available from William Morrow (New York: 1983). The quote by Unamuno is something I ran across on the Internet. The quote by Isaac Pennington is from *Devotional Classics*, edited by Richard Foster (New York: HarperCollins, 1993).

3
Water

The opening quote by Catherine of Siena is from *The Dialogue*, translated by Suzanne Noffke (New York: Paulist Press, 1980), page 366. The closing quote by John Bunyan is from the *The Riches of Bunyan*, updated into today's language by Ellyn Sanna (Uhrichsville, Oh.: Barbour Publishing, 1998), page 75. The final closing quote is by Teresa of Avila in *The Life of Teresa of Jesus*, translated and edited by E. Allison Peers (New York: Doubleday, 1991), pages 189–90, 203.

4

Darkness

Pseudo-Dionysius discusses God's "brilliant darkness" in *The Complete Works,* translated by Colm Luibheid and Paul Rorem (New York: Paulist Press, 1987), pages 127–41. Bonaventure's resplendent, luminous darkness and his other quotes are found in *Bonaventure,* translated by Ewert Cousins (New York: Paulist Press, 1978), page 116. The two passages from John of the Cross can be found in *Lamps of Fire,* edited by Elizabeth Ruth (London: Darton, Longman and Todd, 1985). My copy of *The Cloud of Unknowing* was edited by William Johnston (New York: Doubleday, 1973). Paulist Press published my book *Motherhood: A Spiritual Journey* in 1997. The closing quote by Thomas Merton is from *New Seeds of Contemplation* (New York: New Directions, 1961), page 231.

5

Fire and Light

The opening quote by Catherine of Siena is found in *The Dialogue,* page 366. For further reading on Einstein and light, I recommend *Hyperspace,* by Michio Kaku (New York: Oxford University Press, 1994). The quote by Sir Thomas Browne is from *The Garden of Cyrus,* first published in the seventeenth century. (I found it on the Internet.) Again, the passage from John of the Cross can be found in *Lamps of Fire.* I quoted Rudolfo Llinas from the July 17, 1995, issue of *Time.* The quote by G. K. Chesterton is from an article called "A Piece of Chalk" in *Tremendous Trifles* (London: Dodd, Mead, 1928). The closing quote by Jan van Ruusbroec is found in *Light from Light,* page 187, and the closing quote by Gregory of Nyssa is in *The Lord's Prayer; The Beatitudes,* translated by Hilda C. Graef (Westminster, Md.: Newman Press, 1954), pages 143–44.

6
Tree and Vine

The opening quote by John Bunyan is on page 313 of *The Riches of Bunyan*. The quote from Bernard of Clairvaux's *On the Song of Songs* is taken from M. Basil Pennington's *Bernard of Clairvaux: A Lover Teaching the Way of Love* (Hyde Park, N.Y.: New City Press, 1997), page 116. Sir James George Fraser discusses the ancient meanings of trees in *The New Golden Bough,* Theodor H. Gaster, ed. (New York: S. G. Phillips, 1968), pages 351–52.

7
Food

The opening quote is from *The Dialogue* of Catherine of Siena, previously cited. The quote by Robert Fabing comes from *Real Food: A Spirituality of the Eucharist* (New York: Paulist Press, 1994); Jo Kadlecek's quote is from ther book, *Feast of Life* (Grand Rapids, Mich.: Baker, 1999).

8
Bird

"The Windhover: To Christ our Lord" is in *The Poems of Gerard Manley Hopkins,* 4th edition, W. H. Gardner and N. H. MacKenzie, eds. (New York: Oxford University Press, 1984), page 69; "God's Grandeur" is on page 66. The first closing quote is from *Marian: The Little Arab,* translated by Jean Dumais and Sr. Miriam of Jesus (Eugene, Oreg.: The Carmel of Maria Regina), page 46. The final quote by Margery Kempe is from *The Joy of the Saints,* edited by Robert Llewelyn (Springfield, Ill.: Templegate, 1988), page 149.

Human Metaphors

The quote by John O'Donohue is from his book *Anam Cara* (New York: HarperCollins, 1997).

1

Gardener and Farmer

The opening quote by the seventeenth-century author Ralph Austen is from the preface to his *The Spiritual Use of an Orchard or Garden of Fruit Trees.* I gleaned the poem by Isaac Watts and the Dutch carol that closes this chapter from a book titled *Flora,* an anthology of poetry pertaining to plants compiled by Fiona MacMath (Oxford, England: Lion Publishing, 1990), pages 52, 51. George Herbert, the author of this chapter's first closing quote, was a seventeenth-century poet-priest. He was particularly fond of garden imagery; one of my favorite lines by Herbert is: "I bless thee, Lord, because I GROW."

2

Housewife

The excerpts from George Herbert's poetry are from "Providence" in *George Herbert* (Harmondsworth, England: Penguin Books, 1973), page 87. *Old Dame Counterpane* is by Jane Yolen and illustrated by Ruth Tietjen Councell (New York: Philomel, 1994). The quote by Kierkegaard is yet another quote I jotted down in my journal from some now unknown source. For further thoughts on the nature of time, I recommend Julian Barbour's *The End of Time* (New York: Oxford University Press, 1999). The quote by Santoka I found in Gary Thorp's *Sweeping Changes* (New York: Walker, 2000), pages 25 and 33. The closing quote by Gary Thorp is also from *Sweeping Changes,* the cover copy.

3

The Poor

The opening quote as well as the other quotes by Mother Teresa in this chapter are from *Jesus, the Word to Be Spoken* (Ann Arbor, Mich.: Servant, 1998), pages 32, 39. The opening quote by Francis of Assisi is from *Francis: Bible of the Poor* by Auspicius van Corstanje, translated by David Smith (Chicago: Franciscan Herald, 1977), page 78. The quote by Achiel Peelman is taken from *Christ Is a Native American* (Maryknoll, N.Y.: Orbis, 1995), page 173. Abraham Joshua Heschel's line is quoted in *One Hundred Graces* by Marcia and Jack Kelly (New York: Bell Tower, 1992), page 36.

4
Host

The quote by Anthony Horneck is from *The Crucifixion of Jesus,* published in 1686. It is quoted in the *Oxford English Dictionary,* illustrating an early use of the word *host.* The closing quote by van Corstanje is from *Francis: Bible of the Poor,* page 139.

5
Child

Robert Southwell lived from 1561 to 1595. I found "The Burning Babe" in an Oxford Anthology. The sermon on adolescent girls as a metaphor for God comes from Father Andrew Greeley's novel *Wages of Sin* (New York: Berkeley, 1993). The quote by Angelus Silesius is couplet 103, book 2 from *Cherubic Pilgrim,* translated by H. Plard (Paris: Cerf, 1946).

6
Friend

The opening lines by Bede Jarrett are from one of those quotes I copied in my journal years ago; unfortunately, I don't know the source. The story of the Samaritan woman that opens this chapter's text I based on the Gospel of John, chapter 4. The quote by John Cassian is from his *Conferences,* and the V. Solovyov lines are from *The Meaning of Love.* These quotes, as well as the one from Bonhoeffer's *Life Together,* are all taken from my notebooks of favorite quotes; I don't have more exact bibliographical data. The quotation by Madeleine L'Engle is from *Friends for the Journey* by Madeleine L'Engle and Luci Shaw (Ann Arbor, Mich.: Servant Publications, 1997). My source for Saint Patrick's Breastplate was *A Contemporary*

Celtic Prayer Book by William John Fitzgerald (Chicago: Acta, 1998). The closing quotes by Saint Teresa and Thomas á Kempis are again gleaned from my personal collection of jottings in my journal; I don't know the sources.

7
Bridegroom and Lover

The opening quote is from *Elizabeth of the Trinity,* translated and edited by Conrad de Meester (Paris: Cerf, 1980; Wash., D.C.: Institute of Carmelite Studies, 1984), page 200. The quote from Catherine of Siena is from *The Dialogue,* page 137. Angela of Foligno's quote is from *The Book of Divine Consolation,* translated by Mary G. Steegman (New York: Cooper Square Publishers, 1966), page 162. The quote by Jan van Ruusbroec can be found in *John Ruusbroec: The Spiritual Espousals and Other Works,* translated by James A. Wiseman (New York: Paulist Press, 1985), page 116. The final quote by Mechtild of Magdeburg is from *Swallow's Nest,* Mentioned earlier.

8
Spouse

The opening quote by Angelus Silesius is from the book already referenced, couplet 183, book 1. The quote about *amour courtois* is in an article by Gervase Mathew, "Marriage and *Amour Courtois* in Late Fourteenth-Century England" in *Essays Presented to Charles Williams,* edited by C. S. Lewis (Grand Rapids, Mich.: Eerdmans, 1977), page 131. Teresa of Avila's quote is taken from Camille Campbell's *Meditations with Teresa of Avila* (Santa Fe, N.Mex.: Bear, 1985), page 406. The C. S. Lewis reference is from *Reflections of the Psalms* (New York: Harcourt, Brace, & World, 1958), page 128. The first closing quote is from *Marie of the Incarnation,* edited by Irene Mahoney (New York: Paulist Press, 1989) page 12; the quote by Jan van Ruusbroec is quoted in *Women Mystics* by Louis Bouyer (San Francisco: Ignatius, 1993), page 79; and the final quote by Mechtild of Magdeburg is included in *Swallow's Nest* (previously referenced).

9

Self and Soul

The first opening quote is from *Breakthrough: Meister Eckhart's Creation Spirituality in New Translation,* with introduction and commentaries by Matthew Fox (New York: Doubleday, 1980), page 456. The second opening quote is from *Daily Readings with St. John of the Cross* (Springfield, Ill.: Templegate, 1985), page 43. The story about the six peasants has many versions in Vedantic literature. I adapted this one from Arthur J. Deikman's *The Observing Self: Mysticism and Psychotherapy* (Boston: Beacon, 1982), page 96. The "ghost in the machine" is a phrase from Gilbert Ryle's refutation of Descartes's mind-versus-body dualism; it's found in *The Concept of Mind* (London: Hutchinson, 1949), page 328. The quote by Anthony Bloom is taken from *Ordinary Graces: Christian Teachings on the Interior Life,* edited by Lorraine Kisly (New York: Random House, 2000), page 70. I found Plotinos's quote in Frederick E. Brenk's *Relighting the Soul: Studies in Plutarch, Greek Literature, Religion, and Philosophy* (Stuttgart, Germany: Verlag Stuttgart, 1998), pages 289–90. The long quote from Meister Eckhart is from *Ordinary Graces,* page 138, while the quote from Fénelon is from the same book on the following page. I have summarized Erich Fromm's words on selfishness and self-love found in *The Self,* edited by Clark E. Moustakas (New York: Harper & Row, 1956), pages 58–69. The selection from the Chandogya Upanishad is quoted in *The Voice of the Eagle,* edited and translated by Christopher Bamford (Hudson, N.Y.: Lindisfarne Press, 1990), page 67. Meister Eckhart's discussion of spiritual birthdays is found in *Breakthrough,* pages 303, 309, and 310. The first closing quote is from *Daily Readings with St John of the Cross,* page 65. The closing quote by Anthony Bloom is from *Ordinary Graces,* page 71. The final statement by Rabbi Meir is quoted in *The Sermon on the Mount* by Pinchas Lapides, translated by Arlene Swidler (Maryknoll, N.Y.: Orbis, 1986), page 83.

Conclusion

The opening quote by Joy Davidman (the wife of C. S. Lewis) is from *Smoke on the Mountain* (London: Hodder & Stoughton, 1955). Eckhart's quote is from *Breakthrough: Meister Eckhart's Creation Spirituality in New Translation* (New York: Doubleday, 1980), page 58. Charles Williams was a member of the same writers' group as C. S. Lewis and J. R. R. Tolkien, the Inklings; Williams's novels read like a cross between Dean Koontz and John Bunyan. The quote by Gregory of Nyssa is on pages 94 and 95 of his already quoted book. The Scott London quote is from an article titled "On the Flying Trapeze" in the October 1999 issue of *The Sun*. C. S. Lewis's poem is another one of the many quotes I've collected over the years without complete bibliographical information. The quote by Thérèse of Lisieux can be found on page 80 of *The Autobiography of St. Thérèse of Lisieux* (New York: Doubleday, 1989).